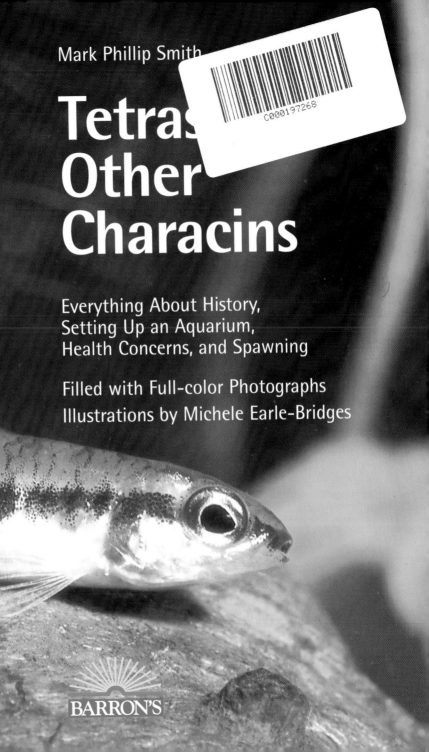

Mark Phillip Smith

Tetras Other Characins

Everything About History, Setting Up an Aquarium, Health Concerns, and Spawning

Filled with Full-color Photographs
Illustrations by Michele Earle-Bridges

BARRON'S

CONTENTS

INTRODUCTION

The order Characiformes encompasses a vast array of subtropical to tropical freshwater fish from both the Old and New World. This order includes the ever-popular tetras as well as their relatives.

What Is Its Name?

Most tropical fish aquarists have kept characins. Characins form a large percentage of tropical fish offered for sale the world over. Aquarists have come to know many of them as small, often brightly colored fish with the name *tetra* attached. However, just what is a tetra? Strictly speaking, the name *tetra* is derived from the subfamily name Tetragonopterinae of the family Characidae. The family Characidae, in turn, is one of 18 families currently residing in the order Characiformes. It is from the order Characiformes that the name *characin* is derived, a more accurate name designation for these popular aquarium fish. Even though those species that reside in the subfamily Tetragonopterinae are the only characins that should technically be referred to as tetras, the name *tetra* has come into common usage in the industry for many years. It is used beyond the species belonging to that subfamily to encompass all the species in the order Characiformes.

This **Hemigrammus ulreyi** *is classified as belonging to the subfamily Tetragonopterinae, thereby making it a tetra in the true sense of the word.*

That being said, many freshwater tropical fish sold and marketed today in the hobby with the name *tetra* as part of their descriptive trade name may not be tetras in the true sense of the word. Thus, the names *tetra* and *characin* have both come into common usage and interchangeably refer to the same order of fish. The author prefers to use the more technically correct name of *characin* when referring to this vast and diverse order of freshwater tropical fish. So as not to bring too much undue confusion among the hobby at large, this book will retain the name *tetra* for whatever trade names are currently being used even though the species in question may not actually belong to the subfamily Tetragonopterinae: that is, the Congo Tetra—*Phenacogrammus interruptus*, the Jelly Bean Tetra—*Ladigesia roloffi*, Splashing Tetras—*Copella* species, Darter Tetras—*Characidium* species and kin, and so on.

So, What Exactly Are Characins?

Characins are classified as primary-division freshwater fish. This means they evolved entirely in a freshwater environment (as opposed to

Most characins are carnivorous, which is exemplified in the mouth structure and dentition of this African Pike Tetra, **Hepsetus odoe.**

Many characins react quickly when food is placed into the aquarium by dashing to the surface to consume the food. This **Astyanax** *species is famous for this behavior.*

secondary-division freshwater fish, whose ancestors evolved from a marine environment). As such, this makes characins very much intolerant of dissolved salts in the water. They usually have well-developed teeth, and most are carnivorous. The upper jaw is usually not protractile. They usually possess an adipose fin and a body usually entirely scaled with ctenoid or ctenoidlike scales. They may have a complete or incomplete lateral line, with some species having a decurved lateral line. They usually have pharyngeal teeth and a caudal fin that typically has 19 rays. Barbels or whiskers are absent. In addition, they lack hard spines in the dorsal and anal fins. Also, as ostiopharyisan fish, they possess the Weberian apparatus. This chain of small bones are connected together and, in turn, connect the air bladder to the internal ear. This enables the fish to hear high-frequency sounds. This structure may also be why these fish seem so skittish in aquariums, as people walk by and make sounds that are acutely audible to them.

These fish also possess chemical alarm systems that consist of pheromones in the skin cells. Injuries to the skin cause these pheromones to be released, which are then detected by the sense of smell, triggering a fright reaction by others of the same species. Some species, particularly the piranhas of the subfamily Serrasalminae, become alarmed at such pheromones. Along with smelling blood in the water, this may trigger their notorious feeding frenzies. These last two features found in characins are said to be useful characteristics for those species that tend to school in large numbers for safety.

So what does this mean to the casual observer or the beginner wishing to start out with characins? Perhaps the easiest way to differentiate characins from other freshwater species found at the local tropical fish dealer is to look for the adipose fin. It is true that some species lack an adipose fin. However, the novice should begin with this and move on to the next criterion. (Catfish also usually have an adipose fin, but they are easily told apart by their barbels or whiskers.) Their bodies are often brightly colored or are primarily silvery. They are usually midwater, active swimmers. Many prefer to school loosely, showing somewhat nervous behavior when startled. They tend to be the first fish to the surface when food is placed into the aquarium, swimming with an active, frenzied pace. In addition to these cursory diagnostic features, the aquarist should become familiar with the huge variety of characin species depicted in chapter 5 of this book as well as in the many quality reference sources on the market. (See the information section at the end of this book.)

Shapes, sizes, colors: Characins come in the most amazing variety of shapes, sizes, and colors that giving further distinguishing features other than those initially mentioned becomes difficult. Some are completely disk shaped, such as that seen in the Silver Dollars—genera *Myleus, Metynnis,* and *Mylossoma,* while others are nearly needle thin, such as *Belonophago tinanti,* and others are every shape in between. Some have the most spectacular colors, such as glowing electric blues and reds seen in the Cardinal Tetra, *Paracheirodon axelrodi*; the silver in some Hatchetfishes, genera *Gasteropelecus, Carnegiella,* and *Thoracocharax*; and the more drab dark gray to black in the Black Pacu, *Colossoma macropomum.* Sizes range from the diminutive Bolivian Pygmy Blue Characin,

A characin's strong sense of smell can often trigger fright or attack responses. Many piranhas, such as this **Serrasalmus geryi,** *are well known for the former response.*

Xenurobrycon polyancistrus, reaching a mere 0.66 inches (17 mm), to the African Tigerfish of the genus *Hydrocynus,* whose species attain a length of 5 feet (150 cm)!

Reproductive strategies: Characins have a bewildering array of reproductive strategies. *Copella arnoldi,* popularly known as the Splashing Tetra, will leap out of the water and deposit their eggs onto an overhanging leaf. *C. arnoldi* recieved its popular name because the male splashes water onto the eggs as they develop.

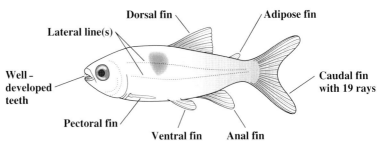

Generalized characin anatomy.

The Cardinal Tetra, Paracheirodon axelrodi, *displays some of the finest coloration to be found in any species of characin.*

Some *Glandulocaudines* possess reproductive glands on their caudal and anal fins, as well as within their gill chambers, that may release odors to attract females. Some species of

It has recently been reported that **Characidium cf. timbuiense** *is capable of climbing up waterfalls. Whether most other* **Characidium** *species, such as this undescribed* **Characidium,** *are capable of this behavior remains to be seen.*

Prochilodontids undertake mass migrations up the Amazon River, much like the North American salmon do, even leaping up waterfalls on their way to spawning grounds.

In regards to feeding strategies, they vary immensely. Tetras and characins can be insectivores, detritivores, planktivores, fin and scale eaters, fish and/or carrion eaters, parasite eaters, or fruit eaters. Additional food categories are being discovered as more research is performed.

Geographic Distribution and Natural Habitats

Characins are found in both the Old and New World. They range from southern Texas down through Central America and into South America, reaching their zenith in species diversity in the Amazon River basin. They are found as far south as Uruguay and the northern half of Argentina. In the Old World, characins are found only on the African continent in virtually all water systems. They are, however, absent from the southern part of the continent and the Sahara Desert. The greatest concentration of species on this continent are found in tropical West and Central Africa. It is estimated that there are between 1,500 and 2,000 species if one includes the undescribed species.

Similar species: Scientists generally accept that, before South America and Africa split apart in the past, characins were already in existence. With the splitting of these two land masses, characins continued to evolve into new species, sometimes along similar pathways. Evidence of this is found in unrelated species that share a similar morphology, ecology, and behavior on both sides of the Atlantic Ocean. The genus *Hepsetus* from Africa appears to be most

Hepsetus odoe *(left) from the African continent is very similar in appearance to South American* **Acestrochynchus** *species (right), indicating a close relationship in the past.*

similar to *Acestrorhynchus* of South America. Some larger *Alestes* species from Africa appear to be similar to some *Brycon* species of South America. Several *Characidium* species of South America share a slender body and bottom-hopping habits with the *Nannocharax* species of Africa. *Citharinus* of Africa appears to be similar to *Prochilodus* and *Curimatus* of South America, not only in overall body shape but also in their detritivorous feeding habits.

Characins have adapted themselves to innumerable biotopes, ranging from diminutive creeks to massive river systems. They can live in stagnant waters such as oxbow lakes, lentic ponds, or large lakes. Some species are capable of developing modified lip extensions in response to poorly oxygenated water, enabling them to absorb what small amounts of oxygen may be available near the sur-

face. Some have adapted to rapids habitats in swiftly flowing rivers, having torpedo-shaped bodies with reduced or absent air bladders. One species of *Characidium* has even been known to climb up waterfalls out of water! In one last example, there exists a blind population of *Astyanax fasciatus*, the Mexican Tetra, that dwells in subterranean water systems of Mexico.

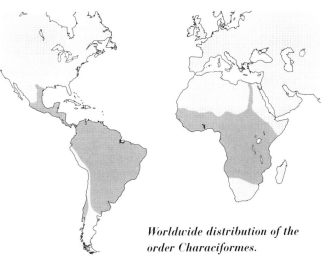

Worldwide distribution of the order Characiformes.

Characin Taxonomy

Characin taxonomy is an evolving science. Within the past ten years, much revealing work has been been undertaken to assess characin relationships better. As of the year 2001, most in the ichthyological community generally accept that there are 18 families. The number of families will surely increase as more investigative work is performed, particularly for those groups, or subfamilies, that currently reside in the family Characidae. This family seems to serve as a catchall grouping for characins. Some of the subfamilies from the family Characidae may eventually be elevated to family status as more thorough studies are performed.

Characin Families

Acestrorhynchidae is endemic to the Amazon River basin. It includes the genera *Acestrorhynchus, Acestrorhamphus, Paroligosarcus*, and *Oligosarcus*. These species are commonly referred to in the hobby as Freshwater Barracudas. All species within this family have tiny scales and pointed snouts studded with numerous unicuspid

It is a possibility that the subfamily Serrasalminae, of which piranhas like this Serrasalmus rhombeus *are a part, will be placed into a separate family in the near future.*

Most species of African Tigerfish, like this Hydrocynus goliath, *are the largest characins known.*

teeth, visible even when the mouth is closed. They are exclusively piscivorous and vary in size from 12 inches (30 cm) to nearly 36 inches (90 cm). All species from this family are imported as juveniles. Since juvenile patterns differ substantially from adult coloration, positively identifying many species is difficult. Juveniles inhabit slow to moderately flowing rivers, whereas adults are found farther away from shore in open water.

Alestidae: This African family was recently split off from the larger family of Characidae. It is in this family that a majority of African species reside. Their size ranges from 1.5 inches (4 cm) to 5 feet (150 cm). Some larger Alestids have scales that approach a diameter of 2 inches (5 cm)! Perhaps the most popular species from this family is the Congo Tetra, *Phenacogrammus interruptus*, a commonly available and very attractive species. The largest species reside in the genus *Hydrocynus*. These are the largest characins known, with several species from this genus attaining a length of 5 feet (150 cm). These characins' food items range from tiny aquatic insects and their larvae to fish. Most species from this family are fairly silvery colored with or without iridescent colors highlighting various parts of the body and fins.

Anostomidae are an exclusively South American family. Their members are commonly encountered in the tropical fish trade. They are marketed as Anostomus and Leporinus, the names of actual genera that are used as popular trade names to refer to many species within this family. The largest species reside in the genus *Leporinus* and can reach a length of nearly 2 feet (60 cm). Most species, however, are much smaller and do not grow beyond 6 inches (15 cm). Many have attractive stripes, spots, or banding along the flanks as juveniles. As they mature, many species loose their appealing juvenile coloration and take on a more drab, greenish brown coloration. Also, many species have strangely shaped, tiny mouths that point upward. Most species are insectivorous or herbivorous.

Characidae has a wide distribution, ranging from southern Texas, through Central America, and into most of South America. It is in this family that a majority of characins reside. This family also has the largest number of subfamilies—13—and is home to the subfamily Tetragonopterina, the true tetras. This family is not monophyletic. In other words, the species in this family are not closely related because they do not derive from a common ancestor. This is a strong indication that this family is an artificial grouping of characins. As more detailed studies are performed on the genera and species of this group, new family names will be erected. These will indicate with better accuracy the actual relationships between the various species. One group likely to split off eventually and be brought to family status is the subfamily Serrasalminae, provenance of the piranhas, silver dollars, and pacus. In fact, some

This unidentified **Anostomus** *species shows the typical body form seen in most Anostomids.*

The Costello Tetra, **Hemigrammus hyanuary,** *is classified as a true tetra.*

This **Bryconamericus** *species collected from the Rio San Juan, in Colonia, Uruguay, resides in the same family as the true tetras, even though it is not a tetra in the true sense of the word.*

Often arriving mixed with shipments of the Spotted Headstander (Chilodus punctatus), *this seldom seen headstander,* Caenotropus maculosus, *sports a different dorsal fin pattern.*

ichthyologists already regard this subfamily as a family unto itself. The verdict is still out, but look for this subfamily to most likely become a family unto itself in the future. Giving a precise categorization of habitat, food preference, and water parameters for this family is difficult since these categorizations span the gamut of all possible parameters known within the order Characiformes.

Chilodontidae are popularly known as Headstanders as they are commonly seen to be swimming in a head-down position. This family is endemic to the Amazon basin. This is a small family (formerly viewed as a subfamily within the family Curimatidae or Anostomidae). It has only two genera and less than a dozen species. The most popular species from this family is the Spotted Headstander, *Chilodus punctatus*. Most species are less than 5 inches (13 cm) long. Natural food items consist of tiny aquatic insects and their larvae.

Citharinidae is an African family comprising large, herbivorous, or detritivorous species found throughout most of the African continent from West to East Africa, up through the Nile River, and through Central Africa. They are the African equivalent to the South American family Prochilodontidae. The largest species can grow to nearly 3 feet (90 cm) and are an important food fish for many African people. Only two genera are represented here, *Citharinus* and *Citharinops*. Most species are silvery colored with tiny scales. Their bodies are very deep, with tiny heads and broad, inferior-shaped snouts. The species of this family are seldom exported for the aquarium trade. The only species that is occasionally exported from time to time is the Rooster Fish, *Citharinus citharus*.

Crenuchidae is found throughout South America. This family contains not only the genera *Crenuchus* and *Poeciliocharax*, but recent genetic analysis has also placed the South American Darter Tetras (genera *Characidium, Ammocryptocharax, Melanocharacidium,* and kin) into this family. These are small fish. The Crenuchids have flashy, complex colors. The South American Darter Tetras, however, typically have cryptic coloration to blend in with their natural environment. The Crenuchids are midwater oriented, while the South American Darter Tetras are primarily bottom oriented. Most species are quite small, typically being under 3 inches (8 cm) long. Some live in slow-flowing rivers and small forest streams and lakes, while others live in torrential environs. *Characidium cf. timbuiense* has recently been documented to scale waterfalls, out of water! The members of this family consume small aquatic insects and their larvae.

Ctenoluciidae are collectively referred to as South American Gars even though this family is in no way closely related to the true gars, the family Lepisosteidae. Some species in this small family can reach a length of approximately

3 feet (90 cm). Perhaps the most commonly imported species to date is *Ctenolucius hujeta*, the common South American Gar. This species can grow to a length of 2 feet (60 cm). Its members are exclusively fish eaters, as can be ascertained by their numerous teeth lining the mouth. Only two genera and half a dozen or so species are known.

Curimatidae is a family endemic to South America. They are small, shy, silvery colored characins that usually do not grow beyond 6 inches (15 cm). Because of their unappealing, silvery coloration, they have garnered few admirers. Many species from differing genera in this family look very similar to one another. This has made it difficult to give an accurate and precise assessment of the number of genera and species. Currently, about eight genera and approximately 100 species are recognized. The species of this family tend toward herbivory.

Cynodontidae: The species of this family were formerly classified as belonging to the family Characidae, subfamily Rhaphiodoninae. Some of the genera recognized as belonging to this family include *Hydrolycus, Rhaphiodon,* and *Cynodon,* which are referred to as Vampire Tetras. This family also includes *Roeboides, Roestes,* and *Gilbertolus,* which are referred to as Glass Headstanders, Longjaw Tetras, and Humpback Characins, respectively. These characins are piscivorous, at least as subadults and adults. Some species are active swimmers. Others, however, "hang out" or typically stay motionless in the same place until nearby prey triggers them to react. Some of the larger species may attain a length of over 3 feet (90 cm). Many species from this family have a completely different color pattern as juveniles, oftentimes being transparent with varying

degrees of black speckling. As they mature, their bodies become less transparent, and the black speckling gives way to a silvery coloration. They are usually found in slow to stagnant backwaters in most river systems of Central and South America but are absent from Chile and the lower half of Argentina.

Distichodontidae is an entirely African family, being found over much of the African continent. This fascinating family contains two subfamilies, Distichodontinae and Ichthyborinae. The most popular and attractive member of the subfamily Distichodontinae is *Distichodus sexfasciatus,* the Six-Barred Distichodus. Species of the subfamily Distichodontinae usually have deep bodies, tiny scales, and very small and narrow, downward pointing mouths. Many have attractive colors as juveniles and adults, while others develop into a grayish brown or silver as they mature. Most species attain a size well over 24 inches (60 cm), although a few reach a length of only 4 inches (10 cm). The subfamily Icthyborinae contains some of the most unusual characins known. They are all elongated predators. Some specifically

Hydrolycus pectoralis is surprisingly sedentary for a fish-eating characin.

Distichodus sexfasciatus *is by far the most attractive of the Distochodontids.*

feed on the fins and scales of other fish, while others are exclusively piscivorous. Some are quite slender. The most elongated characin of all, *Belonophago tinanti*, is from this subfamily. Many species have attractive striping or spotting in their fins. Most species from this subfamily are moderately sized fish, not growing beyond 10 inches (25 cm).

Erythrinidae is an entirely New World family, being found from Costa Rica to most of South America. All the species of this family are preda- tors capable of swallowing fish close to half their size. Some grow to a length of over 4 feet (120 cm) with massive, thick bodies that may be over 12 inches (30 cm) wide. The Erythrinids are the only family where all the species lack an adipose fin. Most species have cryptic col- oration, blending in well among decaying vege- tation and scattered rocks. A few species have attractive colors on their fins and sides of the body. Males generally have longer dorsal fins and more attractive coloration than females.

Gasteropelecidae is a family endemic to the Amazon basin. They are commonly referred to in the hobby worldwide as Hatchetfish due to their greatly expanded, laterally compressed chest.

With straight backs and mouths upturned, these characins are ideally suited for surface dwelling. This is a small family, comprised of three genera and nine species. They range in size from 1 to 3.5 inches (2.5 cm to 8 cm). They are known to fly out of the water to evade predators, much like the marine flying fish of the genus *Exocetus*, although in much shorter distances. In addition to this, they are apparently capable of rapidly moving their pectoral fins to help them glide, or fly, for several yards (meters). Large schools of these characins can be seen simultaneously fly- ing from the water to evade oncoming motor boats, predatory fish, or river dolphins. Typical food items consist of surface-dwelling insects.

Hemiodontidae is another family endemic to the Amazon basin of South America. Hemiodon- tids are delicate, small-scaled species with torpedo-shaped bodies. They are considered open-water dwellers. Most species are silvery colored with various bands or stripes along the length of the body and/or onto the lower lobe or both lobes of the caudal fin. Some possess a single black spot in the middle of the body. Oth- ers may have a swath of white or red coloration next to the black stripe in the caudal fin. The largest species may attain a length of 12 inches (30 cm). However, most that are imported as aquarium fish max out at 6 inches (15 cm). Hemiodontids have a poor survival rate when first captured. Once acclimated, however, they show themselves to be fairly hardy in captivity.

Hepsetidae is an African family consisting of only one species, *Hepsetus odoe*, with the trade name of African Pike Tetra. This species is con- sidered by some to be the most primitive characin. It is exclusively piscivorous, with a for- midable array of teeth lining the mouth even with the mouth completely closed. Any fish too small to be seen as food is typically ignored. One interesting feature of this species has to do with its reproductive strategy. *Hepsetus odoe* is a bubble nest builder much like that seen in labyrinth fish such as gourami, bettas, bush fish, and snake heads. Both parents guard the bubble nest and free-swimming fry for a period of time. The African Pike Tetra inhabits sluggish, swampy areas; lagoons; and flood plains throughout much of its range.

Lebiasinidae: This family consists of two sub-families, the Lebiasininae and the Pyrrhulininae. The subfamily Lebiasininae is comprised of large, 6-inch (15-cm), active, predatory species found throughout South America and into Central America as far north as Costa Rica. The genera from this family are *Lebiasina* and *Piabucina*. They are cylindrical, silver-colored fish with large mouths reminiscent of the Erythrinids. Although not as predatory as the Erythrinids, they are somewhat aggressive and will consume fish and aquatic insects. The subfamily Phyrrhulininae contains the popular Splashing Tetra, *Copella arnoldi,* and its kin. The characins from this sub-family are very popular aquarium fish, especially the Pencilfish, genera *Nannostomus* and *Nanno-brycon.* As aquarium fish go, they are among the most desirable species to maintain. They are small—growing no larger than 2.5 inches (6 cm), colorful, and peaceful. They readily adapt to most prepared aquarium foods. They also do not bother live plants. They are more sensitive than most characins to water conditions, feeling most at home in soft, acidic water. In the wild, Splashing Tetras and Pencilfish consume tiny aquatic insects and their larvae.

Parodontidae are unique, fascinating characins found from southern Central America and throughout most of tropical South America. Up until recently, they were classified as a sub-family of the family Hemiodontidae. They are a small species, seldom reaching over 6 inches (15 cm). Their body form is primarily torpedo shaped and adapted to swimming or darting about the substrate in fast-flowing water. Their swim bladders are reduced to nonexistent, helping to prevent them from being carried away by the current. Another modification for living in swiftly flowing water are modified pectoral fins that act as rudders against the current, forcing them to the substrate. These characins are quite delicate when initially captured and usually die from shock or lack of sufficient oxygen while being transported. However, once in the aquarium, they tend to be rather hardy and undemanding. With their tiny underslung mouths, they are seen to nibble continuously on algae and other tiny organisms on the rocks of their natural habitat.

Prochilodontidae is an exclusively South American family, with the Flagtail Prochilodus, *Semaprochilodus taeniurus,* being the most popular species imported. This family was once considered a subfamily of the family Curimatidae. The Prochildontids are primarily herbivorous or detritivorous. Most attain a length of 12 to 18 inches (30 to 45 cm). Virtually all the species in this family are silver colored, with or without attractive black, yellow, and white banding in the dorsal, anal, and caudal fins. In addition to this, some species may possess red ventral fins. These characins are also popular food fish throughout much of South America due in part to their low oil and fat content, which enables them to be dried and stored for extended periods of time. They are eaten in spite of their muddy tasting flesh and inordinate amount of tiny bones throughout their bodies.

SETTING UP THE AQUARIUM

Before acquiring characins, the new aquarist should be prepared to invest some time to understand the basic husbandry requirements they will require. That way, the hobbyist will be met with success the first time he or she sets up the aquarium.

Aquarium Size and Shape

The habitat preference of characins is quite diverse. They are found in leaf litter, in flooded rain forests, in quiet streams, in swiftly flowing rivers, among aquatic plants, over rocks, over sand, in the open waters of lakes, in swamps, in lagoons, and in subterranean water systems. The pH and water hardness values range widely among these habitats. Having some idea of the characins' natural habitat will help in the aquarist's efforts to prepare and maintain the aquarium.

Giving precise instructions as to the size aquarium one should have for characins is difficult, but a few guidelines can be suggested. The characins typically available in the hobby come in a wide

Chemical filtration is useful for removing pollutants from the water, as well as residual amounts of medications used in the treatment of your characins, like this Astyanax species from Brazil.

variety of sizes. They range from the diminutive Cardinal Tetra, *Paracheirodon axelrodi*, which attains a length of 1.5 inches (4 cm), to the large, bulky Black Pacu, *Colossoma macropomum*, which can grow to 36 inches (90 cm).

If the hobbyist plans to maintain small groups of around 8 to 12 smaller species, such as Cardinal Tetras, Neon Tetras, *P. innesi*, various *Hemigrammus* species and the like, a small aquarium of approximately 15- to 25-gallon (55- to 95-L) capacity will suffice. For a majority of characins, whose average size ranges from 2 to 6 inches (5 to 15 cm), having a larger aquarium with approximately 35- to 100-gallon (130- to 375-L) capacity would be prudent. At the other extreme, if someone chooses to maintain the largest species, such as the Black Pacu—*Colossoma macropomum*, the African Tigerfish—*Hydrocynus* species, or the Banded Leporinus—*Leporinus fasciatus*, to name a few, an aquarium of at least 300 gallons (1,150 L) is the absolute minimum size if they are to grow to adulthood.

Since they are capable of reaching a length of 28 inches (70 cm), these juvenile African Pike Tetras, Hepsetus odoe, will eventually require an aquarium of 300-gallon (1200-L) capacity for long-term successful care.

Approximately 0.5 inch (12 mm) of fish length per 1 gallon (41 L) of aquarium water is a good rule of thumb to follow, at least for the species that do not grow beyond 8 inches (20 cm). This rule of thumb should be multiplied many times over for the largest of characins. The aquarist must be careful, however, in calculating this, since nearly all aquariums sold do not hold the exact number of gallons specified on the label. In order to calculate the volume of water in an aquarium properly, the consumer should measure the interior dimensions of the aquarium in inches (centimeters), multiply the length by the height by the width, and then divide by 231 (946) to get the volume in gallons (liters). The hobbyist should remember that gravel or other furnishings displace some of the water volume, further decreasing the actual volume.

Another factor that will determine the size of the aquarium is the number of fish the aquarist plans on maintaining. That individual should think ahead and decide which species and how many of each he or she plans to maintain, then acquire an aquarium with the appropriate size and shape.

The Aquarium Stand

Aquariums are heavy for their size. A sturdy, stable stand must be provided. Water weighs approximately 8 pounds (18 kg) per gallon. Added to the total weight of the water is the weight of the aquarium and the decorations in it. Not only does the stand need to be sturdy enough to handle all the weight, it also needs to be level so that no one area of the aquarium or stand receives more weight and pressure than necessary. If a stand or aquarium is not completely horizontal, placing a penny or two under the uneven portion of the stand works well.

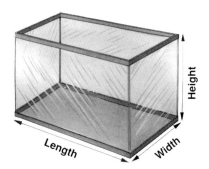

Mathematical equation for calculating the number of gallons of your aquarium: Measure the inside of the aquarium in inches, multiply the width by the height by the length and then divide by 231.

Types of Filtration

Filtration is perhaps the most important aspect of proper aquarium fish husbandry that needs to be understood before one can successfully maintain any fish in the restrictions of a captive environment. In order to maintain fish in an aquarium safely, their water must be filtered (processed). There are three types of aquarium filtration, and using a combination of all three is ideal.

Biological Filtration

The first and most important type of filtration is biological. It is crucial to keeping fish in a closed environment. Without it, maintainig fish in an aquarium is impossible. Any organic material, such as fish waste, uneaten food, decaying plant matter, or dead, rotting fish, is mineralized by heterotrophic bacteria. As a result, ammonia is produced. Ammonia is exceedingly toxic to fish. Additional bacteria further oxidize the ammonia into nitrite. Still other bacteria convert the nitrite to nitrate. This is the nitrification process, or biological filtration in its simplest form.

The initial installation: When a biological filter is first installed, it takes approximately four to six weeks to grow enough bacteria to process the fish's excrement, uneaten food, and decaying plant matter efficiently. A common method employed to begin the four- to six-week maturation process is to use test fish. These can be any species of tropical fish that is extremely hardy and can withstand high concentrations of ammonia and nitrites. Some of the more commonly used, inexpensive, and hardy test fish are the Paradise Gourami—*Macropodus opercularis* and the Blue Gourami—*Trichogaster trichopterus*. These labyrinth fish will normally survive the spike of ammonia and nitrite during the cycling process. Test fish should be maintained and fed daily in the newly set-up aquarium until it has cycled. No water changes should be performed during this period. After the

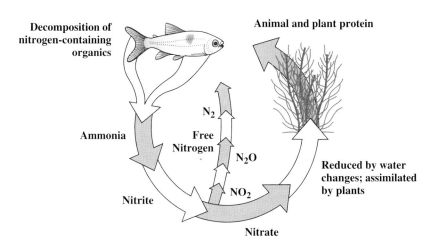

Decomposition of nitrogen-containing organics

Animal and plant protein

Ammonia

N$_2$

Free Nitrogen

N$_2$O

Reduced by water changes; assimilated by plants

Nitrite

NO$_2$

Nitrate

The nitrification process in an aquarium.

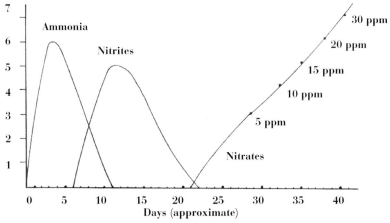

The cycling process of biological filtration.

aquarium has cycled, the aquarist should perform a 50 percent water change, remove the test fish, and add the prized characins.

Monitoring levels: A suitable way to follow the cycling process of the biological filter is to invest in test kits for ammonia, nitrite, and nitrate. The hobbyist should test the newly set-up aquarium daily and monitor any change that takes place. As an alternative, the water can be tested at any reputable tropical fish dealer. Over the course of the first few days, the amount of ammonia in the water will spike. As the ammonia recedes to negligible levels, the nitrites will spike. Then the nitrites will slowly recede to negligible levels as the first nitrate readings occur. When nitrites are no longer present, the aquarium has matured and the cycle is complete.

Acidity: Biological filtration also produces hydrogen ions that lower the pH, making the water more acidic. The easiest way to combat this is to maintain a regular schedule of water changes. Frequent water changes will help to maintain a stable environment for the characins. In addition to preventing the water from

becoming acidic, water changes will help to lower the nitrate levels. The overall well-being of the aquarium residents depends on regularly changing their water.

Chemical Filtration

The second form of filtration is chemical. It may consist of carbon or various pelleted resins used to absorb harmful chemicals from the water. This type of filtration is useful if one lives in an area where the local municipal water supply is contaminated with a variety of chemicals. Chemical filtration is also useful for removing medications from the water after medicines have effected a cure.

Mechanical Filtration

The third form of filtration is mechanical. This form of filtration simply removes visible particulate matter as water passes through a filtering medium so that the water remains free of unsightly sediments.

Whatever form of filtration the hobbyist decides to use, it should biologically filter the water in a consistent and adequate manner, it should also mechanically filter the water to remove visible organic material. Additionally, it should have the capacity to filter the water chemically to remove any harmful chemicals that may be present. The aquarist will need to make sure that the filter does not become clogged with organic material, thereby producing excessive amounts of nitrates. Regularly servicing the filter and performing water changes on a regular basis will help to keep the nitrates low as well as prevent the water from becoming acidic.

Aquarium Water Chemistry

Characins' needs: Characins hail from a variety of water quality parameters. Nevertheless, a majority of characins are found in soft water with a neutral to acidic pH. It may be impossible to duplicate precisely the water chemistry where characins naturally occur. However, the fish keeper can condition the aquarium water in the right direction and, in doing so, achieve a modest facsimile. The pH for characins ranges from about 4.5 to 9.5, with a total mineral hardness ranging from 10 to 150 ppm (parts per million) of carbonate hardness (or 0.5 to 8 kH of German hardness).

Most municipal water comes out of the faucet with a pH of approximately 7.2 to 7.6 and a total mineral hardness that may vary substantially depending on the local water source. If the water supply comes out of the faucet at a neutral pH of 7.0 to 7.2 with low carbonate hardness readings, the water can be used as is. A majority of characins will do just fine in water with a neutral pH with relatively soft water. It is recommended that the aquarist invest in test kits that measure for pH and water hardness. At the least,

Test fish should be used to establish biological filtration so that your prized characins, like this **Xenogoniatus bondi**, *do not have to endure the toxic cycling process.*

the water should be tested at a local retail tropical fish establishment so the characin keeper will be able to determine whether the water needs buffering to increase or decrease the pH and kH.

If the water is too hard and alkaline, a number of things can be done to lower these

For those characins that prefer soft, acidic water, such as this Rummynose Tetra **(Hemigrammus bleheri)**, *every effort should be made to assure that they are provided with the correct water chemistry.*

water parameters. To lower the hardness of the water, the hobbyist should invest in a reverse osmosis unit. This device filters out most of the minerals naturally found in water, thus making it softer. Water passes through a membrane that retains the minerals. The end product of such a device is water with much less mineral content. These devices remove minerals from the water at a slow pace. The unit should be installed so the outtake tube can continuously trickle the soft water into a spare aquarium or large water-holding container. Doing so ensures that a constant supply of soft water will always be available for setting up a new aquarium and, more practically, for doing regular water changes. At this point, acidifying chemicals from a local tropical fish dealer can be added to the water. It is crucial to monitor the amount of acidifying chemicals added to the water. When performing a water change, the new water should have the same pH and kH as that in the aquarium housing the characins. Test kits measuring for pH and kH will be invaluable here. Also, soft water is more subject to a pH crash

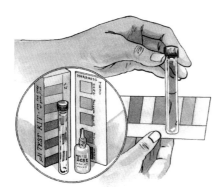

Regular characin maintenance should include testing for pH and hardness.

because of its lack of buffers, providing another reason to monitor the pH and kH regularly.

Alternatively, the aquarist may want to consider maintaining only those species that do not require soft, acidic water to thrive. This means keeping only those species that live in all types of water, as well as those species that come from hard, alkaline water naturally. No matter what kind of water parameters the aquarist has coming from his or her faucet, there will always be those species that are ideally suited to that water.

Another method used to lower the pH and the kH of water is the use of carbon dioxide (CO_2). Specially designed CO_2 devices can be obtained from a local tropical fish establishment and hooked up to supply a constant, slow stream of small CO_2 bubbles into the aquarium. Adding CO_2 into the water in this manner will lower both the pH and kH of the water. The amount will vary depending on the size of the aquarium. So the fish keeper should closely follow the instructions as to how much CO_2 to let seep into the water.

Minimally treated water: If the hobbyist is maintaining species that live in a wide variety of water chemistry parameters in the wild, then water straight from the faucet will suffice. Nothing more needs to be done other than to add a water conditioner to remove any chlorine, chloramine, heavy metals, and other contaminants. The aquarist should remember to add water conditioner to all new water put into the aquarium.

Heater and Thermometer

Characins come from water with a temperature that ranges from about 60°F to 88°F (16°C to 32°C). If the hobbyist lives in an area that experiences very cold winters, then a heater will

If you live in an area with hard water, a reverse osmosis unit may be a necessary device to provide your fish with soft water, especially for characins like this **Hyphessobrycon heraldschultzi.**

For general maintenance purposes, many characins, such as this Congo Tetra, (**Phenacogrammus interruptus**), *readily adapt to most residential tap water, regardless of pH and hardness.*

be needed to maintain the water temperature at a moderate level. If he or she lives in an area that experiences a mild climate year-round, then a heater may not be necessary. The aquarium must be maintained between 74°F and 78°F (23°C and 25°C). If the aquarium is too cool without a heater, then investing in a quality heater will be a must. Aquariums up to 100 gallons (375 L) will probably need only one appropriately sized heater. Much larger aquariums should have two heaters, one at each end of the aquarium, for greater temperature stability.

The hobbyist will need to read the suggested heater size on the heater box before making a purchase. It will give guidelines regarding the size and wattage needed for the aquarium. A general guide to follow is about 3 watts per gallon (1 W per 1.25 L). For example, a 50-gallon (190-L) aquarium would need a 150-watt heater. The heater should be mounted in the aquarium only after it is full of water. The characin keeper needs to wait about half an

hour for the heater's internal thermostat to adjust itself to the temperature of the water before turning on the heater. At this point, an accurate thermometer should be installed.

Lighting

Proper lighting enables the fish keeper to observe the characins more clearly. The main lighting of choice is the fluorescent bulb. However, many characins live in sediment-filled water in their natural habitat, so the amount of light that penetrates their domain is substantially reduced. It is therefore recommended that only one bulb be used. Too much lighting will wash out the colors of these fish, and they will simply not look their best. If live plants are to be maintained along with the characins, there must be sufficient darker areas in the aquarium for the fish to retreat to if they should be frightened. The bulbs should give off white or daylight lighting. Also, characins need to sleep as much as humans do, so the lights should be on only during the day and turned off at night.

Decorations

Determining what kind of decorations to use will depend on what species of characins the hobbyist plans to keep. For most of the smaller species under 6 inches (15 cm), a combination of a few smooth stones scattered about or even submerged African root wood make for a great, natural-looking interior. Using sharp, jagged rocks or wood should be avoided. The characins may injure themselves should they accidentally scrape across them. For species larger than 6 inches (15 cm), the same rock and/or wood combination works well. Note that the aquarium should be less busy with such decorations since larger characins require more swimming space.

Backgrounds are often utilized to make the back of the aquarium look more aesthetically

Remember to turn off your aquarium lights when you go to bed, and to turn them on again when you wake up, because characins, like this undescribed species from the family Characidae, require sleep, too.

pleasing to the eye and to give the characins a better sense of safety. Another option is the use of prefabricated rock or tree root molds designed to be glued onto the inside back of the aquarium. These fiberglass molds provide a realistic decoration for any aquarium.

Substrate and Live Plants

Most fish keepers want to have some sand or gravel in their aquariums. Not only is it pleasing to the eye, it hides the bottom of the aquarium from view. However, having too much sand or gravel will invite bacteria to form anaerobic conditions in the deeper recesses of the gravel bed, so it is advisable not to have too much. On the other hand, if the hobbyist desires to maintain live plants, then having a layer of fine to medium gravel approximately 2 to 3 inches (5 to 8 cm) deep is necessary. An undergravel filter should not be used with live plants.

It is desirable to provide your characins, such as this **Nannostomus espei,** *with a naturally landscaped aquarium. Not only is it pleasing to the eye, but it can provide a closer facsimile to their natural habitat than an aquarium filled with artificially colored gravel and plastic trinkets.*

This **Leporinus arcus** *will require water with a temperature ranging from 74°F to 79°F (23.5°C to 26°C) in order for it to function at its best.*

Java Fern, **Microsorium pteropus,** *is an ideal aquatic plant because it does not require strong lighting to thrive, and because most characins leave this aquatic plant alone.*

Also, when keeping live plants, two aquarium-length, full-spectrum fluorescent bulbs, or those specifically designed for planted aquariums, should be used. The list of possible live plants that can be cultivated in the characin aquarium is far beyond the scope of this introductory guide.

Of course, not all characins can be maintained in a planted aquarium. Those that are herbivores, such as the Silver Dollars, Pacus, and *Distichodus* species to name a few, will make short order of the planted aquarium. For herbivorous characins, a few smooth stones and submerged wood are recommended.

Aquarium Plants

Names and/or genera	Comments
Vallisneria Ceratophyllum Cryptocoryne Echinodoras Microsorium Anubias	Commonly available, easy to maintain
Java moss Vesicularia dubyana	Provides a structure for egg deposition, good for aquarists desiring to spawn their characins
Anubias species Vesicularia dubyana	Can be attached to submerged wood or stones, will take root on them rather than within the gravel

HOW-TO: TYPES OF FILTERS

There are many types of filters on the market. Most do a fair job at maintaining adequate water quality, but some are more efficient than others. The novice should learn about the most popular types before deciding on the best one for his or her characins.

Undergravel Filters

Undergravel filters have long been a very popular filter for both saltwater and freshwater aquariums. A plate is placed under the gravel. Water is drawn down through the gravel by a submersible water pump or air-driven stone, forced through the plate, and circulated back into the aquarium via a tube at the back end of the plate. Bacteria accumulate in the gravel bed so that the gravel bed becomes one big biological filter. These filters provide satisfactory biological filtration initially. Eventually, they become

saturated with organic material and so become nitrate-producing factories. They perform an average job at providing mechanical filtration and provide absolutely no chemical filtration.

Organic material eventually translates into the production of nitrates through the nitrification process, so as much organic material as possible should be removed to keep nitrates to a minimum. With undergravel filters, this is nearly impossible. Over time, this type of filter will collect more organic material than can be removed, particularly below the plates. The result will be the production of high levels of nitrates, regardless of frequent, large-scale water changes and gravel vacuuming.

Trickle Filters

The trickle filter is an excellent biological filter, particularly for filtering large

aquariums. Oxygen saturation is achieved in this filter as the drops of water trickle through the ball-like filter medium. The prefilter serves as the mechanical portion of this filter. A small chamber next to the filter medium is for the chemical-filtering material. Over time, the plastic balls and other internal parts of the filter gather more and more organic material. These, in turn, produce large quantities of nitrates. If the plastic balls are occasionally flushed of their organic buildup and/or a small portion periodically replaced with new plastic balls, excessive amounts of nitrates should not be a problem. Also, as part of regularly maintaining any filter, the aquarist will also need to examine the inside of the filter to make sure it is functioning optimally and remove any buildup of organic material from the walls and floor of the filter as well as from the intake and outtake tubes.

Canister Filters

Canister filters provide biological, chemical, and mechinical filtration. However, they require a lot of servicing if one is to keep the collection of organic material inside the canister to a minimum. They can be difficult and

The sponge filter is ideal for raising juvenile characins. The spongy medium prevents babies from being entrapped.

messy to clean, something that most use as an excuse to put off regular maintenance. Keeping the prefilter clean is important in order not to impede water flow through the canister.

Box Filters

Box filters are capable of providing all three types of filtration but must be serviced frequently in order to keep organic material from building up to the point of producing large amounts of nitrates. Some hobbyists have modified box filters to contain only dime-sized lava rocks in the lower half of the chamber while having a thick piece of sponge on the top half of the chamber. The lava rock provides the surface space for nitrifying bacteria to colonize and thus provide biological filtration. The sponge serves primarily as a prefilter, reducing organic material buildup on the lava rocks. This type of filter seems to work best when the sponge is rinsed thoroughly once a week. It is ideal for aquariums no larger than 30 or 40 gallons (110 to 150 L).

Sponge Filters

Sponge filters are excellent for small aquariums and for raising juvenile fish. The spongy surface is too small to entrap juvenile fish. Eventually, the sponge will break down and will need to be replaced. So the process of reestablishing a biologically mature filter must start again. This can be avoided by starting another sponge filter two months before replacing the old one.

Fluidized Bed Filters

Another type of filter on the market is the fluidized bed filter. This type provides a more efficient biological filtration than those types previously mentioned. Unless a prefilter is

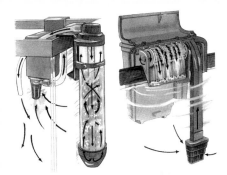

The fluidized bed filter (left) is one of the newest filters on the market; it provides excellent biological filtration. The biological wheel filter (right) is another excellent aquarium filter; it provides all three types of filtration in an efficient arrangement.

attached to the intake valve of a fluidized bed filter, it will provide no mechanical filtration and the fine sand in this filter will eventually clog, reducing its efficiency. This type of filter also does not provide any chemical filtration.

Biological Wheel Filters

The biological wheel filter provides all three types of filtration. This type of filter can be quickly and easily cleaned of its organic buildup without compromising its biological filtering capabilities. This filter has a corrugated wheel situated in the pathway of the water return. As water is returned to the aquarium, it pours over the corrugated wheel, which, once mature, contains the bacteria necessary for biological filtration. This arrangement also enables oxygen to saturate the water, something needed not only by fish but also by the nitrifying bacteria. The back chamber of this filter provides for mechanical and chemical filtration in the form of a filter pad that can easily be replaced before clogging with organic material.

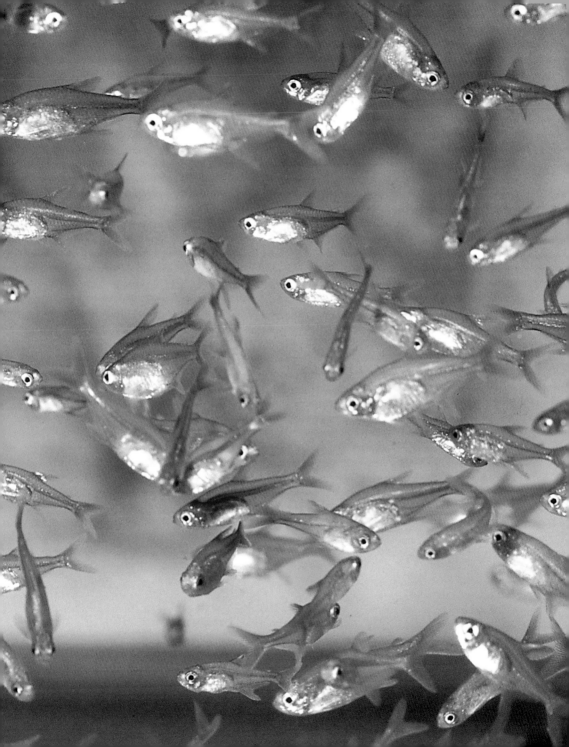

MAINTAINING THE AQUARIUM

Once the characin aquarium has been set up, it must be regularly maintained. Doing so will assure the long-term health of the aquarium inhabitants.

Water Changes

Changing water on a regular basis is the single most important task of aquarium fish keeping. Several factors will determine when, how much, and how often the aquarium water should be changed. The number of characins being maintained, the amount of food fed at each feeding, and how many times daily they are fed will all dictate the water-changing routines. Approximately 25 percent of the volume of the aquarium's water should be changed weekly or 33 percent every two weeks in an aquarium that is sparsely populated (0.5 inch [1.25 cm] of fish per gallon [4 L]). If the characins are crowded (1 to 2 inches [2.5 to 5 cm] of fish per gallon [4 L]), then 40 percent water changes weekly or 60 percent water

When performing your regular water changes on soft water species, such as these Hyphessobrycon amandae, *make sure the new water has the same pH and hardness values, as well as the same temperature.*

changes every two weeks should be standard procedure. These are rough guidelines to follow. Somewhat more or less water may need to be changed depending on the number of fish and the quantity of food given.

Test kits: As previously mentioned, the aquarist should invest in quality test kits. Once the biological filter has cycled, the hobbyist will primarily be testing for nitrate levels. These will indicate when a water change is required. Ideally, the characins should not be exposed to nitrate concentrations beyond 20 ppm (parts per million) for extended periods of time. Many experts agree that long-term exposure to high nitrate levels weaken a fish's immune system and may even subdue or prevent captive reproduction. Most characins can survive high nitrate readings for a while. However, maintaining them in less-than-ideal water conditions over long periods of time is asking for trouble.

Unfavorable water conditions: Characins kept in water with high nitrate levels over an extended period of time may become weakened and unable to resist bacterial or parasitic infections. They may also become more nervous and prone to panic. Characins are typically nervous fish by nature. Maintaining them in less-than-ideal water conditions will cause some to perish over time and others to injure themselves by their nervous, jittery behavior.

How can the fish keeper know if the water changes are keeping the nitrates at an acceptably low level? Before each regular water change, the water should be tested for nitrates. A log of several weeks' readings should be kept. If the readings show that the nitrates are slowly increasing in spite of regular water changes, that will indicate the need for larger and/or more frequent water changes. It may also indicate that the aquarist needs to cut back on the number of fish in the aquarium and the amount he or she is feeding them.

Even though this Red-Bellied Pacu, **Piaractus brachypomum,** *can survive low-oxygen water in the wild for brief periods of time, it is nevertheless strongly recommended that you provide plenty of oxygen to the water at all times.*

Special care should be taken to remove as much detritus as possible with each water change. If an undergravel filter is in place or just a thin layer of gravel is present without an undergravel filter, the characin keeper will need to gravel vacuum the gravel bed during each water change. If using box or power filters, the hobbyist will have to remove the mechanical filtering portion and rinse off the accumulated detritus. These sorts of filters might even have to be thrown away and replaced with a new one. Last, the aquarist may also need to cut back on the amount of food offered to the characins.

The key is to remove as much detritus from the aquarium as quickly as is reasonably possible. The end result of bacterial interaction with detritus is the production of nitrates. If the detritus is allowed to build up, it can truly produce a tremendous amount of nitrates, more so than can be controlled with water changes alone. It is entirely possible that as much as a 90 percent water change can be done in an aquarium and that by the next day or so, the nitrates will be up to their prechange levels if much of the detritus is not removed.

Healthy specimens: It is important to acquire only healthy characins for the aquarium. Even if the species look outwardly healthy (no clamped fins and no scratching on rocks or plants), the water may have elevated levels of nitrates in the dealer's tank. It is not uncommon for some retail establishments, particularly large supermarket-sized pet stores, to maintain their tropical fish in water with high nitrates. It might be advisable to ask what the nitrate level is before purchasing characins. Perhaps the water could be tested before a particular fish is purchased. It is clearly preferable to purchase characins from stores that maintain their specimens in clean, low-nitrate water.

Performing the water change: A siphon hose is an invaluable piece of equipment for performing water changes. Water from the bottom of the aquarium should be siphoned out. If gravel or sand is in the aquarium, a modified siphon hose with a wide mouth at the intake end is recommended. This widened end should be placed into the gravel or sand so that the siphoning action will lift the detritus out while leaving the substrate behind. Because characins are nervous by nature, the aquarist should take special care to perform all aquarium-servicing tasks as quietly as possible and preferably with the lights turned off.

Any new water being placed back into the aquarium should first be thoroughly conditioned with water conditioner from a local tropical fish dealer. Since many characin species prefer soft, acidic water, the new water should be relatively soft and with an acidic to neutral pH. If the hobbyist lives in an area with naturally occurring hard water (with a high mineral content), he or she should use a reverse osmosis device to remove most of the minerals in the water. A reverse osmosis unit does not process large amounts of water in a short time span. It may take it a couple of days to process enough water for a water change. Having the unit installed into a separate water storage tank may be advisable. By the time the reverse osmosis unit has filled the storage tank, the water should be conditioned with peat moss—a substrate that naturally lowers the pH. Alternatively, a high-quality acidifier that is designed to lower the pH can be used. Once the water has been softened, the characin

keeper should attempt to lower the pH to neutral, that is, to 7.0, as a majority of acidic-water-loving characins can adapt to this type of water quality. Before adding this newly conditioned water into the characin aquarium, the water must be tested first. If the new water is not the same quality as that of the aquarium water, further conditioning of the new water

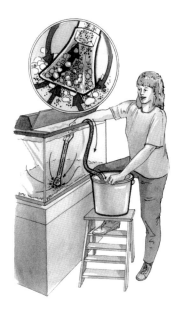

Siphoning water from the aquarium is the most efficient way to perform a water change. If the aquarium is large, siphoning the water out—via a garden hose—into the yard is recommended. For small aquariums, siphon the water into a bucket, then dispense with the water elsewhere. Always siphon from the bottom of the aquarium, particularly if you have an undergravel filter and are using a gravel vacuum.

This omnivorous Ossubtus xinguense *is consuming an algae wafer, thereby providing it with needed vegetable matter.*

may be necessary to get it to match. Last, the temperature of the water should be the same as that of the water within the aquarium and never cooler.

This Red-Bellied Piranha, Pygocentrus nattereri, *should be fed lean beef heart and fresh fish in keeping with its carnivorous diet.*

Aeration

The aquarium water should be saturated with oxygen at all times. Not only do characins need oxygen to survive, so do the bacteria in the biological filter. A clear sign that not enough oxygen is present in the water can be seen when the characins hang out near the top of the aquarium with their mouths touching the surface, gasping for what little oxygen is left. Making sure that enough oxygen is present in the water can be accomplished by the use of an airstone/air pump combination or an outside power filter trickling water back into the tank, agitating the surface.

Diet

In the wild, characins consume a wide variety of foods. The roster of food items is quite substantial and includes other fish, scales and fins of other fish, crabs, shrimp, mammalian flesh, plankton, certain fish parasites, snails, microinvertebrates, algae, plants, seeds, fruit, and mud.

In captivity, most characins will consume a variety of artificially prepared tropical fish foods, whether dried or frozen. That being the case, a large margin of flexibility in what sorts of foods are offered to your characins is reasonable. Nevertheless, the foods that they consume in the wild should be simulated with a reasonable substitute.

Consumers of small fish: For those species that consume primarily small fish or other aquatic animal life, the source of protein offered should be aquatic such as raw fish flesh, shrimps, high-protein frozen or freeze-dried foods, and/or disease- and parasite-free feeder guppies or minnows. However, larger,

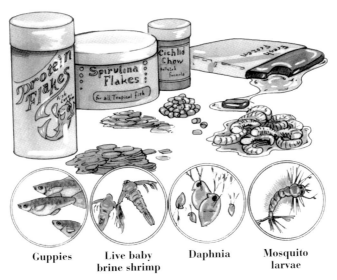

Guppies   Live baby   Daphnia   Mosquito
           brine shrimp   larvae

A varied diet is important for the overall well-being of your characins.

predatory species of the African families Alestidae (genus *Hydrocynus*) and Hepsetidae (genus
Hepsetus) as well as the South American families Acestrorhychidae (genus *Acestrorhychus*),
Characidae (subfamily Rhaphiodontinae, genus
Hydrolycus), Ctenoluciidae (genus *Ctenolucius*),
and Cynodontidae (genus *Cynodontus*) may
accept only live foods. The well-known piranhas (family Characidae, subfamily Serrasalminae, genus *Pygocentrus*) have been
infrequently known to consume wounded
mammals crossing their habitats. In this case,
raw beef heart can be added to their menu.

Most smaller characins under 3 inches (8
cm) consume small aquatic invertebrates in the
water column or from the substrate. These
smaller species relish small, live foods such as
live adult or juvenile brine shrimps, mosquito
larvae, bloodworms, glass worms, daphnia, and

brown worms. These characins can also be
offered a variety of dried and frozen foods
designed for tropical fish.

For herbivorous characins, such as the silver
dollars and red hooks of the family Characidae
(subfamily Serrasalminae, genera *Myleus*,
Mylossoma, and *Metynnis*), as well as most
Distichodontids, there are many high-quality
flake foods on the market with spirulina as a
main ingredient. This food item makes a great
substitute for algae. Inexpensive aquatic plants
like Anacharis, *Elodea* species, or duckweed
(*Lemna minor*) can also be offered as a supplement to their vegetarian diet.

Some unusual food specialists, such as the
scale and fin eaters of the family Distichodontidae (subfamily Ichthyborinae, genera *Phago*,
Paraphago, *Belonophago*, and *Mesoborus*), will
require a constant supply of feeder guppies or

This African Pike Tetra, Hepsetus odoe, *will only accept small live fish as food. Pictured is a sub-adult lunging at its next meal.*

This Distichodus sexfasciatus *is an herbivore and should be provided a diet high in vegetable matter.*

minnows. Some of the species from these genera may also consume the entire fish, while others will eat only the fins or scales.

Most small characins, such as these Cardinal Tetras (Paracheirodon axelrodi)*, and Rummynose Tetra* (Hemigrammus bleheri)*, greedily consume all sorts of aquarium foods, whether live or commercially prepared tablet food.*

Overfeeding: It is highly recommended to take extra care not to overfeed characins. Overfed characins will not look their best, may become lethargic, may lose much of their natural colors, and may cease to show any interest in spawning. They also might grow to hideously large sizes as a result of being fed too much, sizes that they would never reach in the wild. Nothing is more repulsive than an overweight, oversized characin! It is always a good idea to not give characins all they can consume in one feeding. If they are kept slightly hungry, they will always be on the prowl for food and displaying more natural modes of behavior. Additional food preferences for characins can be found described for each species in the chapter "A Representative Section of Tetras and Other Characins."

Parasites and Bacterial Infections

A multitude of parasites and bacterial infections are sporadically encountered in tropical

Be careful not to overfeed your characins, like this **Hydrocynus vittatus,** *as it will eventually lead to health problems and may even hinder spawning.*

Ich is a commonly encountered parasite in the characin aquarium. Notice the small white spots of ich on the tail of this juvenile **Ossubtus xinguense.**

fish, but only a couple seem to be recurrent problems with characins. The easiest thing one can do to minimize the risk of a characin catching a particular ailment, be it a parasitic or bacterial infection, is to practice good husbandry skills. Good husbandry skills will assure a healthy environment for the characin that will, in turn, result in a healthy, vigorous specimen. Only when the needs of the characin are not being met does it begin to become stressed. The immune system of a characin weakens considerably when it becomes stressed and will not be able to fight off an encroaching parasitic or bacterial infection. The result may be that the characin develops a debilitating ailment that will need medicinal treatment if it is to survive. If the characin comes down with parasites or a bacterial infection, the following tips may be helpful. The section entitled "Information" refers the reader to any number of good books about fish disease for additional information.

Ich, or *Ichthyophthirius multifilis,* is probably the most commonly encountered parasite to attack fish in the aquarium. It seems to rear its head when fish are stressed due to a sudden

Neon Tetras, **Paracheirodon innesi,** *seem particularly prone to an infestation of the single-celled parasite called Pleistphora, so much so that this parasitic infestation has been given the moniker Neon Tetra Disease.*

The torn anal fin of this **Roeboides** *species from Uruguay should not be mistaken for fin rot.*

drop in temperature. This parasite may not manifest itself for several days and may attach itself only inside the gills of the host fish. If ich confines itself to the gills, it will be nearly impossible to detect at first. When ich attacks in this manner, it may not be uncommon for the fish to die eventually, seemingly for no apparent reason. At other times, tiny white dots sprinkled over the fish's body, something like the color and size of salt grains, will be seen. Whichever region of the body that ich attacks, the affected fish will probably be seen to glance off objects in an apparent effort to scratch itself.

Fortunately, this is one of the easiest parasitic infections to treat. Malachite green is the most readily available medicine one can use to treat ich. However, some small-scaled characins may be sensitive to this medication. So using a smaller dosage over a longer period of time may be necessary. Ich can have as short as a three-day life cycle depending on the water temperature. So the medicine should be

present in the water for at least three days, four to five being better. It is important to remove any carbon from the filter before using the medicine since the carbon will absorb the medicine, rendering it ineffective. A slight rise in water temperature (to 85°F [30°C]) will help to speed up the life cycle of the ich and help the medicine effect a cure sooner. A 25 percent to 50 percent water change after completing the treatment is advisable along with the addition of fresh carbon to absorb any residual medication that may still be present in the aquarium.

Anchor worm: This parasite, of the genus *Lernaea*, can be seen hanging by its mouth from the characin's body. It is large (for freshwater aquatic parasites) measuring nearly 0.5 inch (12 mm) long. Two dangling appendages can be seen from the back end of the parasite, which are in fact two egg cases. The medication Dimilin works well against this parasite.

When introducing new fish into your aquarium, such as this undescribed characin from the family Characidae, it is recommended that you first quarantine any new purchases for one month before adding them to your primary aquarium.

Treatment may be needed for at least one week. Also, with tweezers, the aquarist should manually remove all anchor worms during treatment.

Neon Tetra disease is caused by a single-celled parasite called *Pleistophora* and seems to affect species from the family Characidae more than other families of characins. As the name implies, Neon Tetras, *Paracheirodon innesi*, are particularly prone. Symptoms include a loss of coloration, erratic swimming, emaciation, deteriorating fins, or a curved spine. Its life cycle, much like ich and velvet, consists of a host stage and a free-swimming stage. Oftentimes, healthy characins may harbor this parasite in small numbers. The fish's natural immune system keeps the parasite in check. However, when characins become stressed, such parasites increase in numbers because the fish's natural immune system decreases. No treatment is successful with this stubborn parasite. Those characins affected should be removed and humanely destroyed.

Fin rot: The bacterial infection called fin rot is evidenced by frayed fins that look as though they have deteriorated away. Fin rot can be treated with any medication on the market that has the drug furazolidone as its active ingredient. The hobbyist must be sure to follow the directions on the package carefully.

Eye infections: Several large-eyed or skittish species of characins may be prone to developing eye infections. This usually begins when the characin scratches its eye against a sharp object in the aquarium. The infection invariably takes hold when the water quality is poor and the injured characin has been stressed for some time. Medications on the market are specially designed to treat eye infections. These have

The quarantine aquarium can also serve as a hospital aquarium for those fish that are unduly harassed in your main aquarium. Make sure that this aquarium is large enough to house any size fish that may need to be moved. This large **Distichodus maculatus** *would require a hospital aquarium with a minimum of 30 gallons (120 L) capacity.*

silver nitrate as the active ingredient. This medication must be applied to the infected eye twice a day. Unfortunately, this means that the fish needing treatment must be removed from the water. One method occasionally used is to remove the characin with the infected eye to a small bucket and add a fish calmer to the container. Once it has become sufficiently drugged, the fish will rest on its side in the container as if dead. At this point, the aquarist must remove it from the container and lay it onto a wet surface. The silver nitrate should be applied according to the instructions. The keeper should then quickly place the fish into another container of water without the calming drug to permit the characin to snap out of its drug-induced torpor. Once the characin has

These Neon Tetras, **Paracheirodon innesi,** *feel more secure and less stressed when kept in an aquarium with their own kind or with other similarly peaceful species.*

Quarantine and Hospital Aquariums

A method often employed by hobbyists and professionals alike is the use of a quarantine aquarium to house newly acquired fish. New characins may be stressed. They may carry a bacterial infection or either internal or external parasites from the dealer's holding tank. If they were to be placed directly into the hobbyist's main aquarium with the other fish, the newly introduced characins might infect the other aquarium inhabitants. This can be a very frustrating experience and is one that all have gone through as novice aquarists.

Aquarium requirements: A quarantine aquarium need only be a 10-gallon (40-L) aquarium for small- to medium-sized species and 30 gallons (110 L) for large specimens. It should have a biological filter up and running such as an outside power filter or an inside sponge filter but no chemical filtration. A heater and thermometer is needed to maintain a constant temperature of 80°F (27°C). A temperature of 85°F (29°C) is needed if treating for ich. There should be no gravel in the aquarium since it will make keeping the aquarium clean during treatment more difficult. The aquarium should not be lit overhead. Enough shelter should be placed into the aquarium so that the quarantined fish will feel safe and secure. If the fish is stressed because it cannot find a place to hide, it may not respond as quickly to treatment. The smaller characin species should be kept with several of their own kind, even while being quarantined, since keeping them in isolation may stress them beyond their ability to respond to treatment. Last, as characins are particularly sensitive to sounds, no one should tap or bang

come to, it should be gently placed back into the main aquarium or back into the hospital aquarium for additional treatments in the following days.

Velvet is caused by the parasitic single-celled organism *Piscinoodinium*. Velvet is also referred to as oodinium. An infected characin will look as though it has been coated in a fine gold dust. If the symptoms of this parasitic infection are caught early, the infected characin can be treated successfully using malachite green or acriflavine. Treatment for this disease is the same as for ich. In addition to medicating the aquarium, raising the water temperature to the mid-eighties helps speed up the life cycle of this parasite and thus effect a cure sooner.

on the aquarium. Doing so will cause the characins to go into an immediate panic.

Length of stay: With a quarantine aquarium set up and running properly, any newly acquired fish should be placed into it for approximately one month. During this time, the quarantined fish is cared for in the same manner as one would for any other aquarium fish. If the fish does have a bacterial infection or parasites, then it will become apparent within a month's time. At first sign of such ailments, the quarantined fish should be treated with the proper medication until it is completely cured. Only then should it be placed into the main aquarium. To remove any leftover medication that may still be present in the quarantine aquarium, carbon (chemical filtration) should be added to the filter.

Double duty: The quarantine aquarium may also double as a hospital aquarium for characins in the main aquarium that become injured or come down with an infection. This way, instead of treating the main aquarium, the fish in question can be removed and placed into the hospital aquarium for individualized treatment.

Adding New Characins to an Established Aquarium

If the hobbyist is considering adding new characins to the aquarium, he or she should make sure that there is plenty of room for more fish. Many of the popular schooling species of the family Characidae (subfamily Characinae, genera *Paracheirodon, Hyphessobrycon, Moenkhausia, Hemigrammus*, and *Gymnocorymbus*) do not mind the addition of other peaceful aquarium residents since these characins feel more secure in a group rather than individually.

Some species, however, are territorial and very aggressive. These include species of the South American family Characidae (subfamily Rhoadsinae, genus *Rhoadsia;* subfamily Characinae, genus *Exodon;* and subfamily Serrasalminae, genera *Ossubtus* and *Acnodon)*; and of the African family Alestidae (genus *Hydrocynus).* In addition, most of these species will require large to very large aquariums to be housed properly. Adding a further specimen to an aquarium already housing these species will likely result in the quick death of the newly introduced individual. It is best to add several of these characins to an aquarium at the same time, and in a sufficiently large aquarium, so that such aggression will be kept to a minimum. If the hobbyist wants to add additional aggressive species to an aquarium that is already firmly established, then he or she should consider setting up another aquarium or two.

Due to the aggressive nature of this **Ossubtus xinguense,** *a large aquarium would be needed to house more than a single specimen together.*

SPAWNING TIPS FOR CHARACINS

Those interested in reproducing characins should start out with the species that are easiest to get to spawn.

Setting the Groundwork

One rewarding facet of maintaining characins is getting them to spawn. Unlike other groups of freshwater tropical fish where a majority of imported species have spawned in captivity, such as live-bearers, killifish, and cichlids, many characins brought into the hobby have yet to reproduce. A number of species, however, are relatively easy to spawn. For the hobbyist willing to expand his or her experience with characins, inducing them to spawn can be a real accomplishment.

Habitats for Spawning

It is challenging to give precise information applicable to most characins as it pertains to

Notice how the male (top) Beckford's Pencilfish, **Nannostomus beckfordi,** *swims along side of the female (bottom) displaying his side to her. This is typical pre-spawning behavior for many characins.*

encouraging them to reproduce in an aquarium. However, a few guidelines can be utilized as a working base. Not all of the characteristics and aquarium parameters listed will apply to all species. A large majority of characin species have not yet reproduced in captivity, so the information given is a rough guide for those species that have reproduced.

Species that have spawned: Generally speaking, those characins that have reproduced for aquarists (species of the genera *Hyphessobrycon, Hemigrammus, Astyanax, Aphyocharax, Ladigesia, Nannostomus, Nannobrycon* and *Nannaethiops*) display an overall similar spawning behavior. Spawning behavior consists of the male and female separating from the group, upon which circling and chasing actions ensue, with the male usually instigating the circling and chasing. After a time of circling and chasing, eggs are scattered onto or about plant roots, leaves, or the substrate among winding channels of rock. In general, there is no parental care of eggs or fry.

A couple of notable exceptions are the Red-Bellied Pirahna—*Pygocentrus nattereri*—and *Rhoadsia altipinna*. Both species care for the eggs and young.

Sexual differences are usually slight to none at all. If there are differences, they usually consist of the male having slightly brighter coloration, tiny hooks on its anal fin (although females of some species have them as well), and more slender bodies and longer fins than females. The anal fin of some males may be shaped differently than that of females. Gravid females will have a fuller appearance than the males. By carefully observing and reading about the characins one desires to spawn over the course of time, becoming familiar with their behaviors toward each other as well as the aforementioned physical characteristics, the aquarist will be able to ascertain which ones are males and which ones are females. This, in turn,

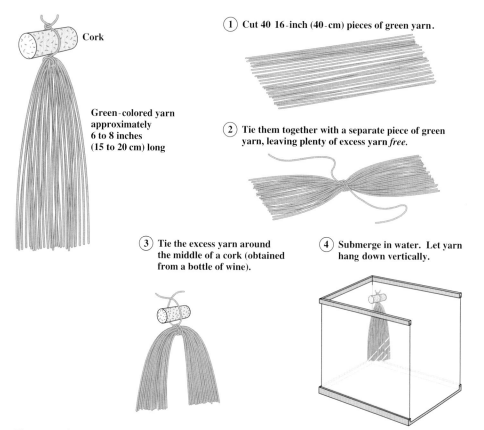

Cork

Green-colored yarn approximately 6 to 8 inches (15 to 20 cm) long

(1) Cut 40 16-inch (40-cm) pieces of green yarn.

(2) Tie them together with a separate piece of green yarn, leaving plenty of excess yarn *free*.

(3) Tie the excess yarn around the middle of a cork (obtained from a bottle of wine).

(4) Submerge in water. Let yarn hang down vertically.

How to make a spawning mop.

will enable the hobbyist to ascertain if he or she has the preferable ratio of at least two females for each male. If the ratio of females to males is off substantially, the excess males should be removed, or additional females should be added.

Preparing the Spawning Aquarium

The spawning aquarium for characins that do not grow to beyond 3 inches (8 cm) can be anywhere between 10 gallons (40 L) and 50 gallons (190 L). The smaller aquarium size should be utilized for the smallest of characins. They should be the only fish in the aquarium. Other fish, if present, may consume any eggs that are deposited. Spawning medium should be a spawning mop, java moss *(Vesicularia dubyana)*, peat, or even smooth, 1-inch (3-cm) gravel covering the bottom of the aquarium. The pH of the water should be lowered to between 6.0 and 7.0 for most species. The hardness of the water should be around 4 to 5 dH. A reverse osmosis unit will do a great job softening the water. The addition of peat into the water will help to acidify the water, lowering the pH to desirable levels. The peat can be put into a nylon bag and allowed to hang into the aquarium or, if a trickle filter is running, into the sump chamber. Adding duckweed *(Lemna minor)* to the spawning aquarium will help to give the characins a better sense of safety and comfort from above. Alternatively, the aquarium lights can be subdued or not used at all.

Last, the characins should be fed the best foods possible. This usually means live foods, such as live brine shrimps (both adult and baby), mosquito larvae, brown worms, bloodworms, tubifex worms, daphnia, or any other small live aquatic foods.

Species That Have Not Yet Spawned in Captivity

Quite a few characin species have not yet reproduced in captivity under natural means. This is mainly due to people not understanding their life cycles in the wild and the various external forces that stimulate spawning. It may also be due to the inability to provide such stimulus in the confines of the home aquarium. For instance, some species of the family Prochilodontidae as well as some of the larger species of the subfamily Serrasalminae migrate over 1,000 miles (1,600 km) up the Amazon River before spawning, something that is impossible to simulate in captivity.

Removing Juveniles to a Separate Aquarium

Once the characins have spawned, the aquarist should consider removing the spawning medium (spawning mop, java moss, peat) to a

The Red-Bellied Piranha, **Pygocentrus nattereri,** *is one of the most commonly spawned piranhas around the world.*

5- or 10-gallon (20- or 40-L) aquarium with water from the original aquarium since the parents may eat many of the eggs. The grow-out aquarium should be spartan, with only a small sponge filter and heater. No overhead lighting is necessary. It is advisable to keep the grow-out tank in a place that does not receive bright, ambient light. Also, the tank should not be filled up to the very top. Instead, the water in it should be about 5 inches (13 cm) deep. This way, as food is added, the minute characin fry will have easier access to the foods being offered without having to swim too far.

Once the tank is set up and the spawning medium with eggs are in place, the hobbyist should continue to observe the aquarium

When rearing tiny juvenile characins, like these Hyphessobrycon amandae, *try lowering the water level so that the juveniles do not have far to go to come into contact with their food.*

carefully for signs of free-swimming fry. The moment he or she sees the first few fry swimming, they should be fed the food items described in the next section. They should receive small amounts three times daily since tiny fry need to be eating more or less constantly during daylight hours, otherwise they may become malnourished and not grow properly. After two to three weeks of feeding the smallest of live foods, such as infusoria, green water, and/or commercially prepared liquid fry foods, the hobbyist can begin to feed them larger live foods such as live baby brine shrimps. Of course, if the newly hatched fry are large enough from the start, the aquarist may be able to begin feeding with live baby brine shrimps and finely crushed flake foods.

First Foods for Newly Hatched Characin Fry

Infusoria: Due to the tiny size of many newly hatched characin young, only the smallest of foods can be consumed. Infusoria is a great live-food option since it is extremely small. When infusoria occur in mass, they look as though the water is misty or smokelike in appearance. The smallest of characin fry can consume this live food. The simplest way to raise infusoria is to fill a 1-gallon (4-L) jar with water and place a few lettuce leaves into it. After a few days, as the lettuce leaves begin to break down, an apple snail (genus *Ampullaria*) should be added to the jar to begin consuming the rotting lettuce. Several days afterward, the small clouds of infusoria forming should begin to be seen. Some should be carefully removed with a small eyedropper and placed directly into the fry tank for immediate consumption.

Due to the tiny size of many characin young, like newly hatched young of the Cardinal Tetra (Paracheirodon axelrodi), infusoria may be the first food they can consume.

Green water: Another food option for newly hatched characins is free-floating, microscopic, single-celled algae. These are more commonly referred to as green water. The characin keeper should set aside a 10-gallon (40-L) aquarium filled with only water and a small air stone to provide a gentle amount of water circulation. The aquarium should be where it will receive at least six hours of direct sunlight per day. Over the course of several days, the water will slowly become green. The point at which one cannot see into the aquarium by 2 inches (5 cm) will indicate that the green water is ready to harvest. The aquarist can simply scoop out 0.5 cup (140 mL) of the green water and gently pour it into the fry tank for immediate consumption.

Commercially prepared liquid foods for juvenile fish: Another food source is the use of commercially prepared liquid food specially designed for juvenile fish. One product that the author has found to work quite well is Liqui-Fresh by Paragon Fish Feed, a branch of Ocean Nutrition. They manufacture a liquid food formula with particles as small as 25 to 50 microns, well under half the size of a newly hatched brine shrimp *nauplii*. The aquarist must remember to shake the bottle before dispensing. He or she should add a couple of drops to a small cup, then add some water to the cup, and stir. Afterward, the contents should be gently poured into the fry tank for immediate consumption.

Live baby brine shrimps: After being fed infusoria, green water, and/or commercially prepared liquid foods for a couple of weeks, the juvenile characins will be large enough to consume live baby brine shrimps.

Another food item for very small characin fry is free-floating algae, or green water. The tiny fry of this Serpae Tetra (Hyphessobrycon equis) would likely benefit from this source of food.

1. Cut four empty 2-liter soda bottles according to the illustration.

2. Invert the longer-cut bottles, and place them upside down into the shorter-cut bottles. Make sure that the lids on the inverted bottles are firmly in place.

3. Fill both inverted containers with water, and add 2 to 3 tablespoons (30 to 45 mL) of rock salt to each. Insert the rigid tubing, connected to an air pump with flexible tubing, into each container all the way to the bottom of the inverted container.

4. Add 1 teaspoon (5 mL) of brine shrimp eggs to only one container.

5. Wait 36 to 48 hours until the water takes on an orange cast. At this point, remove the rigid tubing and allow the eggs and shrimps to settle. The live baby brine shrimps will settle to the bottom of the container.

6. Take another piece of rigid tubing attached to flexible tubing. With the rigid end, siphon the live baby brine shrimps from the bottom of the container into a baby brine shrimp net.

7. Pour the live baby brine shrimps from the baby brine shrimp net into a small container of water.

8. By using an eyedropper, dispense the live baby brine shrimps from the small container.

One day after the first container of brine shrimp eggs hatch, begin the second container following steps 4 through 8. One day after this second container hatches, rinse out the first container and start a new batch as you begin to dispense the live baby brine shrimps from the second container. Repeating

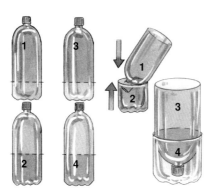

Steps 1 and 2

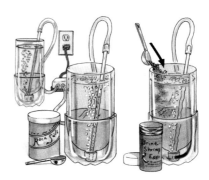

Steps 3 and 4

Hatching brine shrimp eggs.

this procedure will give you a constant supply of live baby brine shrimps for your juvenile characins.

Live baby brine shrimp has recently come back into everyday usage for most hobbyists. This is due to the price of brine shrimp eggs coming down substantially from just a little over a year ago. For a variety of reasons, brine shrimp eggs were as high as $100 per pound until recently, but are now as low as $15 per pound. Since they are so affordable and obtainable, offering live baby brine shrimp to your characin fry once they are large enough to eat them, and even to the adults, is certainly one of the all-time-best small live foods you can offer. For those who have extended experience in spawning tropical fishes, a canister or two of brine shrimp eggs is standard "hardware" that the tropical fish enthusiast is seldom without.

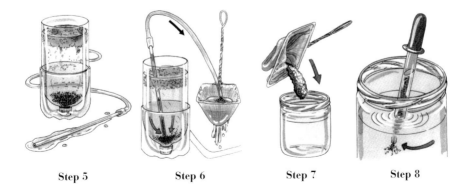

Step 5   Step 6   Step 7   Step 8

A REPRESENTATIVE SELECTION OF TETRAS AND OTHER CHARACINS

Characins come in the most amazing variety of shapes, from disk shaped to pencil shaped. They also display an astonishing range of sizes, from less than 1 inch (3 cm) to over 5 feet (150 cm). On top of that, they possess some of the most striking colors found in any group of freshwater fish.

The classification of characins by family described in this chapter is taken from Dr. Buckup's article "Relationships of the Characidiinae and Phylogeny of Characiform Fishes (Teleostei: Ostariophysi)" published in *Phylogeny and Classification of Neotropical Fishes* in 1998. The species are arranged by continent. African characins are described first, followed by New World species from South and Central America. Within these two broad categories, the species are grouped by their respective families alphabetically. Next, genera and species are arranged within each family alphabetically. Last, when

Males of the African Moon Tetra, Bathyaethiops caudomaculatus, have a more exaggerated humped back and more red pigment than do females.

applicable, their subfamily status is listed after the genus and species name, followed by their common names, if any. A brief discussion is included for all species covered. Information is presented about the name, location and natural habitat, adult size, minimum aquarium size, husbandry, diet, and reproduction.

African Families and Species

Family Alestidae
Name: *Alestes chaperi,* Long-Finned Tetra
Location and Natural Habitat: Guinea to Gabon, West Africa. Inhabits rivers and lakes.
Adult Size: 4 inches (10 cm).
Minimum Aquarium Size: 50 gallons (190 L).
Husbandry: Water chemistry unimportant.

The Long-Finned Tetra, Alestes chaperi, is one of the more attractively adorned species from the genus Alestes.

Male Red Eye Tetras, Arnoldichthys spilopterus, possess rounded, colored anal fins, while the female's anal fin is colorless.

Maintain in groups of six or more. An active species best kept with other active species of similar size. May be overly aggressive to small, shy fish.

Diet: Aquatic insect larvae in the wild. Offer commercially prepared dried and frozen foods supplemented with live mosquito larvae, brine shrimp, brown worms, and daphnia.

Reproduction: Presumably an egg scatterer. Lower pH to 7.0, and dH <10. Provide java moss or spawning mops for spawning medium. Feed juveniles infusoria, liquid fry food, and green water.

Name: *Arnoldichthys spilopterus,* African Red Eye Tetra

Location and Natural Habitat: Niger to Nigeria, West Africa. Inhabits rivers and lakes.

Adult Size: 4 inches (10 cm).

Minimum Aquarium Size: 50 gallons (190 L).

Husbandry Requirements: Water chemistry unimportant. Maintain in groups of six or more. An active species best kept with other active species of similar size. May be overly aggressive to small, shy fish.

Diet: Aquatic insect larvae in the wild. Offer commercially prepared dried and frozen foods supplemented with live mosquito larvae, brine shrimp, brown worms, and daphnia.

Reproduction: An egg scatterer, capable of producing several hundred eggs. Provide java moss or spawning mops for spawning medium. Eggs hatch in 36 hours at 80°F (27°C). Feed juveniles infusoria, liquid fry food, and green water.

Name: *Bathyaethiops caudomaculatus,* African Moon Tetra (See page 48.)

Location and Natural Habitat: Rivers of the Congo Basin, Africa.

Adult Size: 2.5 inches (6.5 cm).

Minimum Aquarium Size: 30 gallons (110 L).

Husbandry Requirements: Water chemistry unimportant. An active species best maintained in groups of at least six in a community aquarium with other peaceful species.

Diet: Aquatic insect larvae in the wild. Offer commercially prepared dried and frozen foods supplemented with live mosquito larvae, brine shrimp, brown worms, and daphnia.

Reproduction: Presumably an egg scatterer. Lower pH to 7.0, and dH <10. Provide java moss or spawning mops for spawning medium. Feed juveniles infusoria, liquid fry food, and green water.

Name: *Bryconaethiops boulengeri*
Location and Natural Habitat: Rivers of the Congo Basin, Africa.
Adult Size: 10 inches (25 cm).
Minimum Aquarium Size: 50 gallons (190 L).
Husbandry Requirements: Water chemistry unimportant. An active, quarrelsome species best maintained in a community setup with similar-sized species.
Diet: Aquatic insect larvae in the wild. Offer commercially prepared dried and frozen foods supplemented with live mosquito larvae, brine shrimp, brown worms, and daphnia.
Reproduction: Unknown. Has not yet spawned in captivity.

Name: *Hemigrammopetersius caudalis*, Yellow Congo Tetra
Location and Natural Habitat: Zaire River and its tributaries in Congo, Africa.
Adult Size: 3 inches (7.5 cm).
Minimum Aquarium Size: 30 gallons (110 L).
Husbandry Requirements: Water chemistry unimportant. An active species, best maintained in groups of at least six in a community aquarium.

Bryconaethiops boulengeri is one of the more streamlined species from the African family Alestidae.

Male **Hemigrammopetersius caudalis** *have white-tipped anal and ventral fins, whereas females do not.*

The Goliath Tigerfish, **Hydrocynus goliath,** *may be the largest of the African Tigerfish, reaching a length of just over 5 feet (1.5 m), and weighing up to 150 pounds (70 kg).*

Diet: Aquatic insect larvae in the wild. Offer commercially prepared dried and frozen foods supplemented with live mosquito larvae, brine shrimp, brown worms, and daphnia.
Reproduction: An egg scatterer, capable of producing several hundred eggs. Lower pH to 7.0, and dH <10. Provide java moss or spawning mops for spawning medium. Feed juveniles infusoria, liquid fry food, and green water.

Name: *Hydrocynus goliath,* Goliath Tigerfish
Location and Natural Habitat: The Congo basin eastward to Lake Tanganyika. Inhabits rivers and lakes.

Adult Size: 5.5 feet (165 cm).

Minimum Aquarium Size: Juveniles and subadults 250 gallons (950 L), adults 2,000 gallons (7,500 L).

Husbandry Requirements: Water chemistry unimportant. Best maintained by itself due to its highly predatory nature.

Diet: Exclusively piscivorous. Offer appropriately sized live fish. May be weaned onto raw fish flesh and shrimp.

Reproduction: Has not yet spawned in captivity.

Name: *Hydrocynus vittatus,* Striped African Tigerfish

Location and Natural Habitat: Found throughout the entire African continent except the Sahara Desert. Inhabits swamps, lakes, and rivers.

Adult Size: 5 feet (150 cm).

Minimum Aquarium Size: Juveniles and subadults 250 gallons (950 L), adults 2,000 gallons (7,500 L).

Husbandry Requirements: Water chemistry unimportant. Best maintained by itself due to its highly predatory nature.

Diet: Exclusively piscivorous. Offer appropriately sized live fish. May be weaned onto raw fish flesh and shrimp.

The Striped Tigerfish, Hydocynus vittatus, *can attain a length and weight approaching that of the Goliath Tigerfish.*

Reproduction: Has not yet spawned in captivity.

Name: *Phenacogrammus interruptus,* Congo Tetra

Location and Natural Habitat: Congo basin, West Africa. Inhabits small, quiet creeks and rivers.

Adult Size: 4.25 inches (11 cm).

Minimum Aquarium Size: 30 gallons (110 L).

Husbandry Requirements: Water chemistry unimportant. An active species best maintained in groups of at least six in a community aquarium with fish of similar size and temperament.

Diet: Aquatic insect larvae in the wild. Offer commercially prepared dried and frozen foods supplemented with live mosquito larvae, brine shrimp, brown worms, and daphnia.

Reproduction: An egg scatterer, capable of producing several hundred eggs. Lower pH to 6.5, and dH <10. Provide java moss, spawning mops, or small smooth stones covering the bottom for spawning. Feed juveniles infusoria, liquid fry food, and green water.

Name: *Phenacogrammus altus*

Location and Natural Habitat: The Congo basin, West Africa. Inhabits small, quiet creeks and rivers.

Adult Size: 3 inches (7.5 cm).

Minimum Aquarium Size: 30 gallons (110 L).

Husbandry Requirements: Water chemistry unimportant for general maintenance. An active species best maintained in groups of at least six in a community aquarium with fish of similar size and temperament.

Diet: Aquatic insect larvae in the wild. Offer commercially prepared dried and frozen foods supplemented with live mosquito larvae, brine shrimp, brown worms, and daphnia.

The ever popular Congo Tetra, Phenaco-grammus interruptus, is a "must have" species for most community aquariums.

Phenacogrammus altus is regularly imported as a byproduct of shipments of the African Moon Tetra.

Reproduction: Unknown. Has not yet spawned in captivity.

Family Citharinidae
Name: *Citharinus citharus*, Rooster Tetra
Location and Natural Habitat: From West Africa to the Nile River. Inhabits various small to large rivers throughout its range.
Adult Size: 2 feet (60 cm).
Minimum Aquarium Size: 150 gallons (600 L).
Husbandry Requirements: Water chemistry unimportant. Best maintained in a community aquarium. May be quarrelsome toward its own kind if not provided with enough space.
Diet: Detritivore, sifting through and consuming organic ooze and plant fragments. Offer commercially prepared aquarium foods high in vegetable content.
Reproduction: Has not yet spawned in captivity.

Family Distichodontidae
Name: *Belonophago tinanti*, subfamily Ichthyborinae
Location and Natural Habitat: Malebo Pool and Ubangui River in the Lower Congo River, Congo, West Africa. Inhabits small creeks and rivers with profuse aquatic vegetation near the shoreline.

The Rooster Tetra, Citharinus citharus, is considered an important food fish throughout Africa.

Adult Size: 6 inches (15 cm).
Minimum Aquarium Size: 50 gallons (190 L).
Husbandry Requirements: Water chemistry unimportant. Best maintained by itself or with

Belonophago tinanti is perhaps the most elongated characin known.

Distichodus affinis *develops a dark gray body coloration as an adult.*

other peaceful aquarium fish at least half its size. Smaller fish will be preyed upon.

Diet: Fins of other fish in the wild. Offer a continuous supply of feeder guppies or shiners as a food source. May consume the entire fish if small enough.

Reproduction: Unknown. Has not yet spawned in captivity.

Name: *Distichodus affinis,* subfamily Distichodontinae

Location and Natural Habitat: Lower Congo basin. Inhabits small creeks and rivers.

Adult Size: 9 inches (22 cm).

Minimum Aquarium Size: 75 gallons (300 L).

This **Distichodus antonii** *often comes mixed in with shipments of juvenile* **Distichodus sexfasciatus.**

Husbandry Requirements: Water chemistry unimportant. An aggressive species that is best maintained in groups of three to four in a community aquarium with other similarly aggressive fish.

Diet: Herbivorous in the wild. Offer commercially prepared foods high in vegetable matter. Supplement the diet with romaine lettuce, peas, and other green vegetables.

Reproduction: Unknown. Has not yet spawned in captivity.

Name: *Distichodus antonii,* subfamily Distichodontinae

Location and Natural Habitat: The Congo basin, West Africa. Inhabits small to moderately sized rivers.

Adult Size: 3 feet (90 cm).

Minimum Aquarium Size: 250 gallons (950 L).

Husbandry Requirements: Water chemistry unimportant. An aggressive species that is best maintained in groups of three to four in a community aquarium with other similarly aggressive fish.

Diet: Herbivorous in the wild. Offer commercially prepared foods high in vegetable matter. Supplement the diet with romaine lettuce, peas, and other green vegetables.

Reproduction: Unknown. Has not yet spawned in captivity.

Name: *Distichodus decemmaculatus,* subfamily Distichodontinae

Location and Natural Habitat: The Congo basin, West Africa. Inhabits quiet creeks and small rivers with lush aquatic vegetation.

Adult Size: 4 inches (10 cm).

Minimum Aquarium Size: 40 gallons (150 L).

Husbandry Requirements: Water chemistry unimportant. A shy, aggressive species that is best maintained in groups of three to four in a

Distichodus decemmaculatus *is a rare* Distichodus *species that occasionally finds its way into the hobby.*

community aquarium with other similarly aggressive fish.

Diet: Herbivorous in the wild. Offer commercially prepared foods high in vegetable matter. Supplement the diet with romaine lettuce, peas, and other green vegetables.

Reproduction: Unknown. Has not yet spawned in captivity.

Name: *Distichodus fasciolatus,* subfamily Distichodontinae

Location and Natural Habitat: From Cameroon to Angola, West Africa. Inhabits small to moderately sized rivers.

Distichodus fasciolatus, *like most species of the genus* Distichodus, *needs a high vegetable content diet for long-term successful care.*

Adult Size: 2 feet (60 cm).

Minimum Aquarium Size: 250 gallons (950 L).

Husbandry Requirements: Water chemistry unimportant. An aggressive species that is best maintained individually in a community aquarium with other similarly aggressive fish.

Diet: Herbivorous in the wild. Offer commercially prepared foods high in vegetable matter. Supplement the diet with romaine lettuce, peas, and other green vegetables.

Reproduction: Unknown. Has not yet spawned in captivity.

Name: *Distichodus lussoso,* subfamily Distichodontinae

Location and Natural Habitat: The Congo basin, West Africa. Inhabits small to moderately sized rivers.

Adult Size: 16 inches (40 cm).

Minimum Aquarium Size: 250 gallons (950 L).

Husbandry Requirements: Water chemistry unimportant. An aggressive species that is best maintained individually in a community aquarium with other similarly aggressive fish.

Diet: Herbivorous in the wild. Offer commercially prepared foods high in vegetable matter.

Distichodus lussoso *is considered to be one of the more aggressive* Distichodus, *capable of holding its own in an aquarium with aggressive cichlids.*

Distichodus sexfasciatus is the most attractive and popular Distichodus species. It will retain its attractive orange coloration if fed a diet high in vegetable matter and carotene-rich foods.

Supplement the diet with romaine lettuce, peas, and other green vegetables.

Reproduction: Unknown. Has not yet spawned in captivity.

Name: *Distichodus sexfasciatus*, subfamily Distichodontinae)

Location and Natural Habitat: The Congo basin, West Africa. Inhabits small to moderately sized rivers.

Adult Size: 3 feet (90 cm).

Minimum Aquarium Size: 250 gallons (950 L). Can be maintained in much smaller aquariums as a juvenile and subadult.

Husbandry Requirements: Water chemistry unimportant for general maintenance. An aggressive species. Best to maintain this species with large, predatory, aggressive fish.

Diet: Herbivorous in the wild. Offer commercially prepared foods high in vegetable matter. Supplement the diet with romaine lettuce, peas, and other green vegetables.

Reproduction: Unknown. Probably an egg scatterer. Has not yet spawned in captivity.

Name: *Ichthyborus ornatus,* subfamily Ichthyborinae

Location and Natural Habitat: Congo River basin. Inhabits creeks and small rivers.

Adult Size: 8.5 inches (18 cm).

Minimum Aquarium Size: 50 gallons (190 L).

Husbandry Requirements: Water chemistry unimportant. Best maintained by itself or with other peaceful aquarium fish at least half its size. Smaller fish will be preyed upon.

Diet: Fins of other fish in the wild. Offer a continuous supply of feeder guppies or shiners as a food source. May consume the entire fish if small enough.

Reproduction: Unknown. Has not yet spawned in captivity.

Name: *Nannaethiops unitaeniatus,* subfamily Distichodontinae

Location and Natural Habitat: Nigeria to the Congo Basin. Inhabits small creeks and rivers.

Adult Size: 2.5 inches (6.5 cm).

Minimum Aquarium Size: 15 gallons (55 L).

Husbandry Requirements: Water chemistry unimportant. An active species best maintained in groups of at least six in a community aquarium with other small, peaceful fish.

Diet: Aquatic insect larvae in the wild. Offer commercially prepared dried and frozen foods

Ichthyborus ornatus is one of the few fin-eating characins in the aquarium hobby.

Male **Nannaethiops unitaeniatus** *are slender with reddish highlights on the body, whereas females are more robust and lack red pigment.*

The African Pike Tetra, Hepsetus odoe, *is one of only a couple of characin species that builds bubble nests, much like Labyrinth Fishes.*

supplemented with live mosquito larvae, brine shrimp, brown worms, and daphnia.

Reproduction: Presumably an egg scatterer. Provide soft, acidic water (pH 6.5/dH 5) and plenty of java moss or spawning mops for egg deposition. Feed juveniles infusoria, liquid fry food, and green water.

Name: *Neolebias trewavasae*, subfamily Distichodontinae

Location and Natural Habitat: Congo River basin. Inhabits creeks and small rivers.

Adult Size: 2.5 inches (6.5 cm).

Minimum Aquarium Size: 20 gallons (75 L).

Neolebias trewavasae *is beginning to make a comeback in the hobby after an absence of several years.*

Husbandry Requirements: Water chemistry unimportant. An active species best maintained in groups of at least six in a community aquarium with other small, peaceful fish.

Diet: Aquatic insect larvae in the wild. Offer commercially prepared dried and frozen foods supplemented with live mosquito larvae, brine shrimp, brown worms, and daphnia.

Reproduction: Presumably an egg scatterer. Provide soft, acidic water (pH 6.5/dH 5) and plenty of java moss or spawning mops for egg deposition. Feed juveniles infusoria, liquid fry food, and green water.

Family Hepsetidae

Name: *Hepsetus odoe*, African Pike Tetra

Location and Natural Habitat: Found from West to Central Africa southward to the Zambezi River, Zimbabwe. Inhabits rivers, lakes, and swamps.

Adult Size: 28 inches (70 cm).

Minimum Aquarium Size: 150 gallons (600 L).

Husbandry Requirements: An excellent show fish. Can be kept with other large predatory species provided there is ample space. Do not maintain with fish half its size, as they will be preyed upon.

Diet: Exclusively piscivorous. Offer live guppies and minnows.

Reproduction: Has not yet spawned in captivity. A bubble nest builder. The bubble nest, approximately 2 inches (5 cm) thick and 8 inches (20 cm) in diameter, is constructed in shallow, quiet water among tall aquatic grasses. Eggs (0.1 inch [2.5 mm] in diameter) are deposited in the foam. Both male and female guard the nest until the eggs hatch. Some parental care afterward. Has yet to be seriously worked with in captivity. Best attempted in a pond.

South and Central American Families and Species

Family Acestrorhynchidae

Name: *Acestrorhynchus altus*, South American Barracuda Tetra

Location and Natural Habitat: Paraguay and Amazon River basin. Inhabits slow-flowing rivers and oxbow lakes.

Adult Size: 15 inches (38 cm).

Minimum Aquarium Size: 100 gallons (375 L).

Husbandry Requirements: Water chemistry unimportant. A nervous species best kept in an

Acestrorhynchus altus is one of the more commonly imported South American Barracuda tetras.

This juvenile Acestrochynchus cf. nasutus possesses markedly different coloration than as an adult. The horizontal stripes become much less prominent with age.

open aquarium without decorations. Can be maintained with most other moderately peaceful fish provided they are too large to be swallowed whole.

Diet: Exclusively piscivorous. Offer live guppies or minnows.

Reproduction: Unknown. Has not yet spawned in captivity.

Name: *Acestrorhynchus cf. nasutus*, South American Barracuda Tetra

Location and Natural Habitat: Guyana and Amazon River basins. Inhabits slow-flowing rivers and oxbow lakes.

Adult Size: 12 inches (30 cm).

Minimum Aquarium Size: 100 gallons (375 L).

Husbandry Requirements: Water chemistry unimportant. A nervous species best kept in an open aquarium without decorations. Can be maintained with most other moderately peaceful fish provided they are too large to be swallowed whole.

Diet: Exclusively piscivorous. Offer live guppies or minnows.

Reproduction: Unknown. Has not yet spawned in captivity.

Family Anostomidae

Name: *Abramites hypselonotus,* Headstander

Location and Natural Habitat: Orinoco and Amazon Rivers and their tributaries. Inhabits fast-flowing streams and rivers.

Adult Size: 6 inches (15 cm).

Minimum Aquarium Size: 55 gallons (210 L).

Husbandry Requirements: Water chemistry unimportant. Provide plenty of current. Pile up wood and smooth stones to create places where it can retreat to. Gets along with most other aquarium fish, yet may nip the fins of long-finned species.

Diet: Herbivorous in the wild. Offer commercially prepared foods high in vegetable matter. Supplement diet with romaine lettuce, peas, and other green vegetables.

Reproduction: Unknown. Has not yet spawned in captivity.

Name: *Anostomus anostomus,* Anostomus

Location and Natural Habitat: Amazon River basin. Inhabits fast-flowing, shallow streams and rivers, spending much time within channels created by rocks.

Adult Size: 7 inches (17.5 cm).

Minimum Aquarium Size: 55 gallons (210 L).

The Headstander, Abramites hypselonotus, is a great beginner's characin for those looking for something a little out of the ordinary.

Male Anostomus anostomus have more red in the dorsal fin and thicker golden banding along the midline of the body than females.

Husbandry Requirements: Water chemistry unimportant. Does best in a group with its own kind rather than individually. Provide plenty of current. Pile up wood and smooth stones to create places where it can retreat to. Gets along with most other aquarium fish, yet may nip the fins of long-finned species.

Diet: Herbivorous and insectivorous in the wild. Offer commercially prepared foods high in vegetable matter. Supplement diet with romaine lettuce, peas, and other green vegetables as well as with brine shrimp, brown worms, daphnia, and mosquito larvae.

Reproduction: Lower pH to 7.0 and dH <10. Courtship commences with both male and female in a head-down, vertical position. Lays adhesive eggs that are scattered among rocks or vegetation. Feed juveniles infusoria, liquid fry food, and green water.

Name: *Anostomus taeniatus* (See page 17.)

Location and Natural Habitat: Amazon River basin. Lives underneath thickly vegetated areas of slow-flowing rivers.

Adult Size: 8 inches (20 cm).

Minimum Aquarium Size: 75 gallons (300 L).

Husbandry Requirements: Prefers soft (dH <5), acidic (pH 6.5) water. A peaceful species that does best in a group of its own kind.

Provide submerged wood and various smooth stones for hiding places. Gets along with most other aquarium fish if they are not too small.

Diet: Herbivorous in the wild. Offer commercially prepared foods high in vegetable matter. Supplement the diet with romaine lettuce, peas, and other green vegetables.

Reproduction: Unknown. Has not yet spawned in captivity.

Name: *Leporinus affinis,* Banded Leporinus

Location and Natural Habitat: Amazon River basin. Inhabits swift-flowing streams and rivers over sandy and rocky bottoms.

Adult Size: 12 inches (30 cm).

Minimum Aquarium Size: 100 gallons (375 L).

Husbandry Requirements: Water chemistry unimportant. Provide plenty of current along with submerged wood and various smooth stones. Can be maintained with other large, aggressive aquarium fish if they are of the same size.

Diet: Herbivorous in the wild. Offer commercially prepared foods high in vegetable matter. Supplement the diet with romaine lettuce, peas, and other green vegetables.

Reproduction: Unknown. Has not yet spawned in captivity.

The Banded Leporinus, Leporinus affinis, can grow to a respectable size of 12 inches (30 cm), something to keep in mind when purchasing a much smaller juvenile.

The Three-Spot Anostomus, Pseudanos trimaculatus, displays noticeable red lips, typical for this species.

Name: *Pseudanus trimaculatus,* Three-Spot Anostomus

Location and Natural Habitat: Guyana and the Amazon River basin southward through the Mato Grosso. Inhabits a variety of biotopes from swamps, lakes, and slow-flowing streams and rivers over vegetated or sandy, rocky bottoms.

Adult Size: 5 inches (12.5 cm).

Minimum Aquarium Size: 40 gallons (150 L).

Husbandry Requirements: Water chemistry unimportant. Provide submerged wood and various smooth stones for hiding places. Can be maintained with other peaceful aquarium fish if they are of the same size and temperament.

Diet: Herbivorous and insectivorous in the wild. Offer commercially prepared foods high in vegetable matter. Supplement the diet with small amounts of live or frozen, high-protein foods.

Reproduction: Unknown. Has not yet spawned in captivity.

Family Characidae

Name: *Acnodon normani,* Sheep Pacu, subfamily Serrasalminae

Location and Natural Habitat: Tocantins and Xingu Rivers in Brazil. Inhabits rocky riffles with scattered sandy patches.

The Xingu River of Brazil is home to a large number of unusual characin species, such as this Sheep Pacu, Acnodon normani.

The Bloodfin Tetra, Aphyocharax anisitsi, *is a great beginner's characin to attempt to spawn.*

Adult Size: 16 inches (40 cm).

Minimum Aquarium Size: 150 gallons (600 L).

Husbandry Requirements: Water chemistry unimportant. A robust, hardy, and active swimming species. An extremely aggressive characin that is best maintained with other aggressive species larger than itself. Do not maintain with smaller, less aggressive species.

Diet: Omnivorous in the wild. Offer a varied diet consisting of commercially prepared dried and frozen foods that include algae or spirulina. Supplement the diet with live brown worms, mosquito larvae, daphnia, and bloodworms.

Reproduction: Unknown. Has not yet spawned in captivity.

Name: *Aphyocharax anisitsi,* Bloodfin Tetra, subfamily Aphyocharacinae

Location and Natural Habitat: The Rio Parana, Argentina. Inhabits quiet, slow-flowing rivers among aquatic vegetation.

Adult Size: 2 inches (5 cm).

Minimum Aquarium Size: 10 gallons (40 L).

Husbandry Requirements: Water chemistry unimportant. Provide submerged wood and various aquatic plants. A peaceful species best maintained with other non-aggressive species of

similar size. Prefers cooler water temperature 70°F to 72°F (21°C to 22°C).

Diet: Aquatic insect larvae and plankton in the wild. Offer commercially prepared dried and frozen foods supplemented with live mosquito larvae, brine shrimp, brown worms, and daphnia.

Reproduction: Condition adults on live foods. Provide spawning mops or java moss as a spawning medium. Remove adults after spawning, or remove spawning mop or java moss with eggs to a separate aquarium. Feed juveniles infusoria, liquid fry food, and green water.

Name: *Aphyocharax paraguayensis,* White-Spot Tetra, subfamily Aphyocharacinae

Location and Natural Habitat: Rio Paraguay basin. Inhabits quiet, slow-flowing rivers among aquatic vegetation.

Adult Size: 1.5 inches (4 cm).

Minimum Aquarium Size: 5 gallons (20 L).

Husbandry Requirements: Prefers acidic (pH 6.5), soft (dH <5) water. Provide submerged wood and various aquatic plants. A peaceful species best maintained with other nonaggressive species of similar size.

Diet: Aquatic insect larvae and plankton in the wild. Offer commercially prepared dried and

As the species name implies, **Aphyocharax paraguayensis** *is found within the Rio Paraguay basin of South America.*

frozen foods supplemented with live mosquito larvae, brine shrimp, brown worms, and daphnia.

Reproduction: Condition adults on live foods. Provide spawning mops or java moss as a spawning medium. Remove adults after spawning, or remove spawning mop or java moss with eggs to a separate aquarium. Feed juveniles infusoria, liquid fry food, and green water.

Name: *Astyanax fasciatus,* Blind Tetra, subfamily Tetragonopterinae

Location and Natural Habitat: Mexico to northern Central America. Inhabits small creeks and streams. The blind form (pictured) is found in subterranean waters.

Adult Size: 3.5 inches (8.5 cm).

Minimum Aquarium Size: 30 gallons (110 L).

Husbandry Requirements: Water chemistry unimportant. Prefers cool water, 65°F to 68°F (18°C to 20°C). Provide plenty of open space, as it is an active swimmer. A peaceful species best maintained with other nonaggressive species.

Diet: Omnivorous in the wild. Offer commercially prepared dried and frozen foods that include spirulina. Supplement diet with live brown worms, mosquito larvae, daphnia, and bloodworms.

Reproduction: Water chemistry unimportant. Provide spawning mops or java moss as a spawning medium. Remove adults afterward, or remove spawning mop or java moss with eggs to a separate aquarium. Offer newly hatched juveniles live baby brine shrimp.

Name: *Boehlkea fredcochui,* Blue Tetra, subfamily Tetragonopterinae

Location and Natural Habitat: Peru and Columbia. Inhabits quiet, sluggish creeks with aquatic vegetation.

Adult Size: 2 inches (5 cm).

Minimum Aquarium Size: 10 gallons (40 L).

Husbandry Requirements: Water should be somewhat acidic, with a pH of 6.5 to 7.0, and

The subterranean blind form of Astyanax mexicanus *is the only blind species of tropical fish regularly available to hobbyists.*

The Blue Tetra, Boehlkea fredcouchui, *displays more subtle blue hues than many characins.*

Because the Sickle-Band Brycon, **Brycon melanopterus,** *is one of the larger characins imported for the aquarium hobby; it would be an ideal display characin in a large aquarium.*

dH <10. A peaceful species best maintained with its own kind or with other small, peaceful aquarium fish.

Diet: Aquatic insect larvae and crustaceans in the wild. Offer commercially prepared aquarium foods, both dry and frozen. Supplement diet with live brine shrimp, mosquito larvae, daphnia, and brown worms.

Reproduction: Reported as reproducing in captivity but without detailed information. Probably similar to *Astyanax fasciatus*.

Name: *Brycon melanopterus*, Sickle-Band Brycon, subfamily Bryconinae

Location and Natural Habitat: Amazon River basin. Inhabits rivers, oxbow lakes, and swamps.

Adult Size: 10 inches (25 cm).

Minimum Aquarium Size: 75 gallons (300 L).

Husbandry Requirements: Water chemistry unimportant. Best maintained in a school of four to six. Keep aquarium sparsely decorated as this species needs a lot of swimming space. A peaceful species but may chase after much smaller species.

Diet: Omnivorous in the wild. Offer a variety of commercially prepared dried and frozen foods that include spirulina. Supplement diet with live mosquito larvae, brine shrimp, brown worms, and daphnia.

Reproduction: Unknown. Has not yet spawned in captivity.

Name: *Bryconodon* sp., subfamily Bryconinae

Location and Natural Habitat: Amazon River basin. Inhabits rivers, oxbow lakes, and swamps.

Adult Size: 12 inches (30 cm).

Minimum Aquarium Size: 100 gallons (375 L).

Husbandry Requirements: Water chemistry unimportant. An aggressive species best maintained with other large, aggressive fish. Keep interior of aquarium sparsely decorated as this species needs a lot of swimming space. Do not maintain with any fish small enough to be considered as food.

Diet: Piscivorous in the wild. Offer live guppies or minnows supplemented with fresh-frozen, high-protein foods.

Reproduction: Unknown. Has not yet spawned in captivity.

This unidentified **Bryconodon** *species is predatory, and should not be maintained with smaller fish unable to withstand its aggressiveness.*

The Wimple Piranha, Catoprion mento, *is notorious for eating the scales and fins of smaller tankmates.*

The Black Pacu, Colossoma macropomum, *can live up to 65 years.*

Name: *Catoprion mento,* Wimple Piranha, subfamily Serrasalminae

Location and Natural Habitat: Guyana through Brazil to the Mato Grosso. Inhabits sluggish creeks, rivers, swamps, and stagnant ponds.

Adult Size: 6 inches (15 cm).

Minimum Aquarium Size: 55 gallons (210 L).

Husbandry Requirements: Water chemistry unimportant. A hardy, active swimming species that is best maintained by itself since it may feed on the scales of its tank mates. If fed enough, it may abandon its scale- and fin-eating habits. If maintained with other species, make sure they are larger.

The Pink-Tail Chalceus, Chalceus macrolepidotus, *is the more commonly imported* Chalceus *species. Both species are easy to care for provided they are given ample swimming space.*

Diet: Consumes the scales and fins of other fish in the wild. Readily adapts to all sorts of prepared aquarium foods, both dried and frozen. Supplement the diet with live feeder guppies.

Reproduction: Unknown. Has not yet spawned in captivity.

Name: *Chalceus macrolepidotus,* Pink-Tail Chalceus, subfamily Characinae

Location and Natural Habitat: Amazon River basin. Inhabits most river systems.

Adult Size: 10 inches (25 cm).

Minimum Aquarium Size: 80 gallons (300 L).

Husbandry Requirements: Water chemistry unimportant. A hardy, active species best maintained with other large fish of similar temperament. A jumper—keep the lid tightly covered.

Diet: Piscivorous in the wild. Adapts to all sorts of aquarium foods. Diet should be predominantly protein based, whether frozen, live, or dried.

Reproduction: Unknown. Has not yet spawned in captivity.

Name: *Colossoma macropomum,* Black Pacu, subfamily Serrasalminae

Location and Natural Habitat: Amazon River basin. Inhabits nearly all types of aquatic habitats.

Adult Size: 40 inches (100 cm).

Minimum Aquarium Size: 300 gallons (1,150 L).

Husbandry Requirements: Water chemistry unimportant. Provide plenty of open space, as this species is an active swimmer. Best maintained in a small school or with other large, nonaggressive species.

Diet: Omnivorous, with a preference for seeds in the wild. Offer a varied diet consisting of commercially prepared dried and frozen foods. Supplement diet with soft fruits.

Reproduction: Unknown. Has not yet spawned in captivity.

Name: *Exodon paradoxus,* Buck-Toothed Tetra, subfamily Characinae

Location and Natural Habitat: Amazon River, Brazil, French Guyana, and Guyana. Inhabits most small to moderately sized river systems.

Adult Size: 6 inches (15 cm).

Minimum Aquarium Size: 80 gallons (300 L).

Husbandry Requirements: Water chemistry unimportant. A very active and aggressive species that is best maintained with larger, aggressive species. Do not maintain with smaller, peaceful species.

Diet: Piscivorous, insectivorous, and also eats scales and fins in the wild. Offer high-protein foods such as live feeder guppies, fresh shrimp, frozen foods, and pellets.

Reproduction: Condition adults on live foods. Lower pH to 6.5 to 7.0 and dH <10. Provide spawning mops or java moss as a spawning medium. Remove adults afterward, or remove spawning mop or java moss with eggs to a separate aquarium. Feed juveniles infusoria, liquid fry food, and green water.

Name: *Gymnocorymbus ternetzi,* Black Skirt Tetra, subfamily Tetragonopterinae

Location and Natural Habitat: Rio Paraguay and Rio Guapore, Bolivia, as well as the rivers of southern Brazil. Inhabits quiet, sluggish creeks with aquatic vegetation.

Adult Size: 2.5 inches (5.5 cm).

Minimum Aquarium Size: 15 gallons (55 L).

Husbandry Requirements: Water chemistry unimportant. A peaceful species best maintained with its own kind or with other small, peaceful aquarium fish.

Diet: Aquatic insect larvae and crustaceans in the wild. Offer commercially prepared aquarium foods, both dry and frozen. Supplement diet with live brine shrimp, mosquito larvae, daphnia, and brown worms.

For those hobbyists looking for a scrappy characin, try the Buck-Toothed Tetra, **Exodon paradoxus.**

The Black Skirt Tetra, **Gymnocorymbus ternetzi,** *is one of the most highly recommended species for beginning aquarists.*

A school of Rummynose Tetras, **Hemigram-mus bleheri,** *in a planted aquarium makes for a spectacularly beautiful feast for the eyes.*

Reproduction: Water chemistry unimportant. Provide spawning mops or java moss as a spawning medium. Remove adults afterward, or remove spawning mop or java moss with eggs to a separate aquarium. Offer newly hatched juveniles live baby brine shrimp.

Name: *Hemigrammus bleheri,* Rummynose Tetra, subfamily Tetragonopterinae
Location and Natural Habitat: Rio Vuapes, Columbia, and Rio Negro, Brazil. Inhabits quiet, sluggish creeks with aquatic vegetation.
Adult Size: 1.75 inches (4.5 cm).
Minimum Aquarium Size: 15 gallons (55 L).
Husbandry Requirements: Water should be acidic, pH 6.5 to 7.0, and dH <5. A peaceful species best maintained with its own kind or with other small, peaceful aquarium fish.
Diet: Aquatic insect larvae and crustaceans in the wild. Offer commercially prepared aquarium foods, both dry and frozen. Supplement diet with live brine shrimp, mosquito larvae, daphnia, and brown worms.
Reproduction: Will spawn among java moss or spawning mops on the bottom of the aquarium. Remove parents after spawning. Eggs hatch and are completely free-swimming after the fourth day at a temperature of 78°F (26°C).

Offer juveniles infusoria and green water as first foods.

Name: *Hemigrammus erythrozonus,* Glowlight Tetra, subfamily Tetragonopterinae
Location and Natural Habitat: Essequito River, Guyana. Inhabits quiet, sluggish creeks with aquatic vegetation.
Adult Size: 1.5 inches (3.5 cm).
Minimum Aquarium Size: 5 gallons (20 L).
Husbandry Requirements: Water chemistry unimportant. A peaceful, active species best maintained in a school of at least eight or with other tiny, peaceful aquarium fish.
Diet: Aquatic insect larvae in the wild. Offer commercially prepared aquarium foods, both dry and frozen. Supplement diet with live brine shrimp, mosquito larvae, and daphnia.
Reproduction: Raise the temperature to 84°F (29°C), and reduce the lighting. Provide java moss or spawning mops as a place for the eggs to be deposited. After spawning, remove parents. Offer newly hatched young infusoria and green water as a first food.

The Glowlight Tetra, **Hemigrammus erythrozonus,** *one of the mainstays of the aquarium hobby, is a hardy species and an attractive aquarium resident.*

The golden hue on the body of the Gold Tetra, **Hemigrammus rodwayi,** *is from a substance secreted by the skin to protect it against parasites. Captive-reared individuals do not show this attractive golden hue.*

Name: *Hemigrammus rodwayi,* Gold Tetra, subfamily Tetragonopterinae

Location and Natural Habitat: Guyana. Inhabits quiet, sluggish creeks and lakes with aquatic vegetation.

Adult Size: 2 inches (5.0 cm).

Minimum Aquarium Size: 10 gallons (40 L).

Husbandry Requirements: Water chemistry unimportant. A peaceful, active species best maintained in a school of at least eight or with other tiny, peaceful aquarium fish.

Diet: Aquatic insect larvae in the wild. Offer commercially prepared aquarium foods, both dry and frozen. Supplement diet with live brine shrimp, mosquito larvae, and daphnia.

Reproduction: Maintain pH between 6.5 to 7.0, and dH <10. Will spawn among java moss or spawning mops on the bottom of the aquarium. Remove parents after spawning. Offer juveniles infusoria and green water as a first food.

Name: *Hemigrammus ulreyi,* Ulrey's Tetra, subfamily Tetragonopterinae

Location and Natural Habitat: Upper Paraguay River system. Inhabits moderately flowing small rivers.

Adult Size: 2 inches (5 cm).

Minimum Aquarium Size: 10 gallons (40 L).

Husbandry Requirements: Water chemistry unimportant. A peaceful, active species best maintained in a school of at least eight or with other tiny, peaceful aquarium fish.

Diet: Aquatic insect larvae in the wild. Offer commercially prepared aquarium foods, both dry and frozen. Supplement diet with live brine shrimp, mosquito larvae, and daphnia.

Reproduction: Unknown. Has not yet spawned in captivity.

Name: *Hyphessobrycon amandae,* Amanda's Tetra, subfamily Tetragonopterinae

Location and Natural Habitat: Amazon River basin in Brazil. Inhabits quiet, sluggish creeks and lakes with aquatic vegetation.

Adult Size: 1.25 inches (3 cm).

Minimum Aquarium Size: 5 gallons (20 L).

Husbandry Requirements: Prefers soft (dH <5), acidic (pH 6.5 to 7.0) water. A peaceful, active species best maintained in a school of at least eight or with other tiny, peaceful aquarium fish.

Diet: Aquatic insect larvae in the wild. Offer commercially prepared aquarium foods, both dry and frozen. Supplement diet with live brine shrimp, mosquito larvae, and daphnia.

Ulrey's Tetra (**Hemigrammus ulreyi**) *is one of the more subtly colored characins that, when maintained in a school, seem to become more attractive.*

Amanda's Tetra (**Hyphessobrycon amandae**) *was named after the mother of famed tropical fish collector Heiko Bleher.*

Reproduction: Unknown. Has not yet spawned in captivity.

Name: *Hyphessobrycon bentosi*, Rosy Tetra, subfamily Tetragonopterinae

Location and Natural Habitat: Guyana and the Amazon River basin. Inhabits quiet, sluggish creeks and lakes with aquatic vegetation.

Adult Size: 2 inches (5 cm).

Minimum Aquarium Size: 10 gallons (40 L).

Husbandry Requirements: Prefers soft (dH <5), acidic (pH 6.5 to 7.0) water. A peaceful, active species best maintained in a school of at least eight or with other tiny, peaceful aquarium fish.

Diet: Aquatic insect larvae in the wild. Offer commercially prepared aquarium foods, both dry and frozen. Supplement diet with live brine shrimp, mosquito larvae, and daphnia.

Reproduction: Will spawn among java moss or spawning mops on the bottom of the aquarium. Remove parents after spawning. Offer juveniles infusoria and green water as a first food.

Name: *Hyphessobrycon equis*, Serpae Tetra, subfamily Tetragonopterinae

Location and Natural Habitat: Southern Amazon River basin and Paraguay River. Inhabits quiet, sluggish creeks and lakes with aquatic vegetation.

Adult Size: 1.75 inches (4 cm).

Minimum Aquarium Size: 10 gallons (40 L).

Husbandry Requirements: Prefers soft (dH <5), acidic (pH 6.5 to 7.0) water. A peaceful, active species best maintained in a school of at least eight or with other tiny, peaceful aquarium fish. May nip at long-finned species.

Diet: Aquatic insect larvae in the wild. Offer commercially prepared aquarium foods, both dry and frozen. Supplement diet with live brine shrimp, mosquito larvae, and daphnia.

The Rosy Tetra (**Hyphessobrycon bentosi**) *is not as commonly available as the more brilliantly colored* **Hyphessobrycon species** *currently in the hobby.*

The Serpae Tetra (**Hyphessobrycon equis**) *comes highly recommended for those looking for a small, colorful, and peaceful aquarium fish for small aquariums.*

Hyphessobrycon colombianus is one of the newer Hyphessobrycon species in the hobby, and has been met with much acclaim.

Reproduction: Will spawn among java moss or spawning mops on the bottom of the aquarium. Remove parents after spawning. Offer juveniles infusoria and green water as a first food.

Name: *Hyphessobrycon colombianus*, subfamily Tetragonopterinae
Location and Natural Habitat: Ecuador. Inhabits quiet, sluggish creeks and lakes with aquatic vegetation.
Adult Size: 2 inches (5 cm).
Minimum Aquarium Size: 10 gallons (40 L).

The actual meaning of the species name of the Bleeding Heart Tetra, (Hyphessobrycon erythrostigma) is "red spot" in reference to the "bleeding heart" spot on the side of its body.

Husbandry Requirements: Prefers soft (dH <5), acidic (pH 6.5 to 7.0) water. A peaceful, active species best maintained in a school of at least eight or with other tiny, peaceful aquarium fish.
Diet: Aquatic insect larvae in the wild. Offer commercially prepared aquarium foods, both dry and frozen. Supplement diet with live brine shrimp, mosquito larvae, and daphnia.
Reproduction: Will spawn among java moss or spawning mops on the bottom of the aquarium. Remove parents after spawning. Offer juveniles infusoria and green water as a first food.

Name: *Hyphessobrycon erythrostigma*, Bleeding Heart Tetra, subfamily Tetragonopterinae
Location and Natural Habitat: Western Amazon basin in Brazil and Peru. Inhabits quiet, sluggish creeks and lakes with aquatic vegetation.
Adult Size: 2.75 inches (7 cm).
Minimum Aquarium Size: 20 gallons (75 L).
Husbandry Requirements: Prefers soft (dH <5), acidic (pH 6.5 to 7.0) water. A peaceful, active species best maintained in a school of at least eight or with other tiny, peaceful aquarium fish.
Diet: Aquatic insect larvae in the wild. Offer commercially prepared aquarium foods, both dry and frozen. Supplement diet with live brine shrimp, mosquito larvae, and daphnia.
Reproduction: Will spawn among java moss or spawning mops on the bottom of the aquarium. Remove parents after spawning. Offer juveniles infusoria and green water as a first food.

Name: *Hyphessobrycon pulchripinnis*, Lemon Tetra, subfamily Tetragonopterinae
Location and Natural Habitat: Central Brazilian Amazon River basin. Inhabits quiet, sluggish creeks and lakes with aquatic vegetation.

Hyphessobrycon pulchripinnis *was given the trade name Lemon Tetra due to the yellow coloration in its fins.*

Adult Size: 2 inches (5 cm).

Minimum Aquarium Size: 10 gallons (40 L).

Husbandry Requirements: Prefers soft (dH <5), acidic (pH 6.5 to 7.0) water. A peaceful, active species best maintained in a school of at least eight or with other tiny, peaceful aquarium fish.

Diet: Aquatic insect larvae in the wild. Offer commercially prepared aquarium foods, both dry and frozen. Supplement diet with live brine shrimp, mosquito larvae, and daphnia.

Reproduction: Will spawn among java moss or spawning mops on the bottom of the aquarium. Remove parents after spawning. Offer juveniles infusoria and green water as a first food.

The Flameback Tetra (Hyphessobrycon pyrrhonotus) *is one of the more recently described species from the genus* Hyphessobrycon.

Name: *Hyphessobrycon pyrrhonotus,* Flameback Tetra, subfamily Tetragonopterinae

Location and Natural Habitat: Rio Negro, Brazil. Inhabits quiet, sluggish creeks and lakes with aquatic vegetation.

Adult Size: 2.5 inches (6 cm).

Minimum Aquarium Size: 20 gallons (75 L).

Husbandry Requirements: Prefers soft (dH <5), acidic (pH 6.5 to 7.0) water. A peaceful, active species best maintained in a school of at least eight or with other tiny, peaceful aquarium fish.

Diet: Aquatic insect larvae in the wild. Offer commercially prepared aquarium foods, both dry and frozen. Supplement diet with live brine shrimp, mosquito larvae, and daphnia.

Reproduction: Will spawn among java moss or spawning mops on the bottom of the aquarium. Remove parents after spawning. Offer juveniles infusoria and green water as a first food.

Name: *Metynnis argenteus,* Silver Dollar, subfamily Serrasalminae

Location and Natural Habitat: Amazon River basin east of the Rio Negro. Inhabits nearly all types of aquatic habitats.

Adult Size: 6 inches (15 cm).

Minimum Aquarium Size: 75 gallons (300 L).

Husbandry Requirements: Water chemistry unimportant. Provide plenty of open space, as this species is an active swimmer. Best maintained in a school of at least eight. Can be maintained with other peaceful aquarium fish.

Diet: Herbivorous in the wild. Offer a variety of commercially prepared and frozen foods high in vegetable content. Supplement the diet with inexpensive live aquatic plants, romaine lettuce, and peas.

Reproduction: Lower pH to 7.0, dH <10, and reduce lighting. Spawns in groups. Provide

Metynnis argenteus is commonly referred to in the hobby as a Silver Dollar. Other Metynnis *species bear this common name as well.*

Metynnis lippincottianus, commonly known as the Spotted Silver Dollar, is better maintained in a school than individually.

spawning mops or water hyacinth as a spawning medium. Remove adults afterward, or remove spawning mop or water hyacinth with eggs to a separate aquarium. Eggs hatch in three days at a temperature of 80°F (27°C). Feed juveniles infusoria, liquid fry food, and green water.

Name: *Metynnis lippincottianus,* Spotted Silver Dollar, subfamily Serrasalminae
Location and Natural Habitat: Amazon River basin. Inhabits nearly all types of aquatic habitats.
Adult Size: 6 inches (15 cm).
Minimum Aquarium Size: 75 gallons (300 L).
Husbandry Requirements: Water chemistry unimportant. Provide plenty of open space, as this species is an active swimmer. Best maintained in a school of at least eight. Can be maintained with other peaceful aquarium fish.
Diet: Herbivorous in the wild. Offer a variety of commercially prepared and frozen foods high in vegetable content. Supplement the diet with inexpensive live aquatic plants, romaine lettuce, and peas.
Reproduction: Treat the same as for *Metynnis argenteus.*

Name: *Moenkhausia pittieri,* Diamond Tetra, subfamily Tetragonopterinae
Location and Natural Habitat: Lake Valencia and surrounding rivers in Venezuela.
Adult Size: 2.5 inches (6.5 cm).
Minimum Aquarium Size: 15 gallons (55 L).
Husbandry Requirements: Prefers soft (dH <5), acidic (pH 6.5 to 7.0) water. A peaceful, active species best maintained in a school of at least eight or with other tiny, peaceful aquarium fish.
Diet: Aquatic insect larvae in the wild. Offer commercially prepared aquarium foods, both dry and frozen. Supplement diet with live brine shrimp, mosquito larvae, and daphnia.

The Diamond Tetra (**Moenkhausia pittieri**) *is perhaps the most elegant* **Moenkhausia** *species known.*

Reproduction: Will spawn among java moss or spawning mops on the bottom of the aquarium. Remove parents after spawning. Offer juveniles infusoria and green water as first foods.

Name: *Moenkhausia sanctaefilomenae,* Amazon Red-Eye Tetra, subfamily Tetragonopterinae
Location and Natural Habitat: Peru-Brazil border area through Paraguay and eastern Bolivia. Inhabits quiet, sluggish creeks and lakes with aquatic vegetation.
Adult Size: 2.5 inches (6.5 cm).
Minimum Aquarium Size: 15 gallons (55 L).
Husbandry Requirements: Prefers soft (dH <5), acidic (pH 6.5 to 7.0) water. A peaceful, active species best maintained in a school of at least eight or with other tiny, peaceful aquarium fish.
Diet: Aquatic insect larvae in the wild. Offer commercially prepared aquarium foods, both dry and frozen. Supplement diet with live brine shrimp, mosquito larvae, and daphnia.
Reproduction: Reduce overhead lighting. Will spawn among java moss or spawning mops on the bottom of the aquarium. Remove parents after spawning. Offer juveniles infusoria and green water as first foods.

The Amazon Red-Eye Tetra, (Moenkhausia sanctaefilomenae) *is another great beginner's characin to attempt to spawn.*

Myleus pacu *is a seldom seen species in the hobby. As it grows, the juvenile shown here will grow into a large, gray fish reminiscent of the Black Pacu,* Colossoma macropomum.

Name: *Myelus pacu,* subfamily Serrasalminae
Location and Natural Habitat: Amazon River basin east of the Rio Negro. Inhabits nearly all types of aquatic habitats.
Adult Size: 2 feet (60 cm).
Minimum Aquarium Size: 200 gallons (750 L).
Husbandry Requirements: Water chemistry unimportant. Provide plenty of open space, as this species is an active swimmer. Although timid when young, *M. pacu* becomes more extroverted with age. Best maintained with several of its own kind or with other large, nonaggressive species from the same subfamily.
Diet: Omnivorous, with a preference for seeds in the wild. Offer a varied diet consisting of commercially prepared dried and frozen foods. Supplement diet with soft fruit.
Reproduction: Unknown. Has not yet spawned in captivity.

Name: *Myleus rubripinnis,* Red Hook Met, subfamily Serrasalminae
Location and Natural Habitat: Amazon River basin. Inhabits nearly all types of aquatic habitats.
Adult Size: 8 inches (20 cm).
Minimum Aquarium Size: 100 gallons (375 L).

The Red Hook Met (**Myleus rubripinnis**) *is certainly one of the more popular Silver Dollar–like characins commonly imported for the aquarium trade.*

Husbandry Requirements: Water chemistry unimportant. Provide plenty of open space, as this species is an active swimmer. Best maintained in a school of at least eight. Can be maintained with other peaceful aquarium fish.

Diet: Herbivorous in the wild. Offer a variety of commercially prepared and frozen foods high in vegetable content. Supplement the diet with inexpensive live aquatic plants, romaine lettuce, and peas.

Reproduction: Lower pH to 7.0, dH <10, and reduce lighting. Spawns in groups. Male has

Myleus schomburgki *shows much variation in the width and length of its vertical bar.*

more exaggerated anal fin. Provide spawning mops or water hyacinth as a spawning medium. Remove adults afterward, or remove spawning mop or water hyacinth with eggs to a separate aquarium. Eggs hatch in three days at a temperature of 80°F (27°C). Feed juveniles infusoria, liquid fry food, and green water.

Name: *Myleus schomburgki*, Schomburgk's Silver Dollar, subfamily Serrasalminae
Location and Natural Habitat: Amazon River basin of Brazil and Venezuela. Inhabits nearly all types of aquatic habitats.
Adult Size: 5 inches (12.5 cm).
Minimum Aquarium Size: 75 gallons (300 L).
Husbandry Requirements: Water chemistry unimportant. Provide plenty of open space, as this species is an active swimmer. Best maintained in a school of at least eight. Can be maintained with other peaceful aquarium fish.
Diet: Herbivorous in the wild. Offer a variety of commercially prepared and frozen foods high in vegetable content. Supplement the diet with inexpensive live aquatic plants, romaine lettuce, and peas.
Reproduction: Unknown. Has not yet spawned in captivity.

Name: *Nematobrycon palmeri*, Emperor Tetra, subfamily Tetragonopterinae
Location and Natural Habitat: Western Columbia. Inhabits quiet, sluggish creeks and lakes with aquatic vegetation.
Adult Size: 2 inches (5 cm).
Minimum Aquarium Size: 15 gallons (55 L).
Husbandry Requirements: Prefers soft (dH <5), acidic (pH 6.5 to 7.0) water. A peaceful, active species best maintained in a school of at least eight or with other tiny, peaceful aquarium fish.

This captive-reared Emperor Tetra (Nematobrycon palmeri) shows a greater degree of blue coloration than that found in wild populations.

One of the newer and more unusual characins to have come into the hobby is this Ossubtus xinguense, commonly known as the Eagle Beak Pacu or Parrot Pacu.

Diet: Aquatic insect larvae in the wild. Offer commercially prepared aquarium foods, both dry and frozen. Supplement diet with live brine shrimp, mosquito larvae, and daphnia.

Reproduction: Reduce overhead lighting. Will spawn among java moss or spawning mops on the bottom of the aquarium. Remove parents after spawning. Offer juveniles infusoria and green water as first foods.

Name: *Ossubtus xinguense*, Eagle Beak Pacu, Parrot Pacu, subfamily Serrasalminae

Location and Natural Habitat: Endemic to the lower Xingu River, Brazil. Habitat consists of moderately flowing water with rocks, boulders, and sandy areas.

Adult Size: 10 inches (20 cm).

Minimum Aquarium Size: 100 gallons (375 L).

Husbandry Requirements: Water chemistry unimportant. A robust, hardy, and active swimming species. This species is one of the most aggressive characins known, particularly toward fish that look similar to itself or of similar size. Should be kept by itself or with aggressive species larger than itself. However, it generally ignores tiny tetras, barbs, and catfish.

Diet: Omnivorous in the wild. Offer a varied diet consisting of commercially prepared dried and frozen foods.

Reproduction: Unknown. Has not yet spawned in captivity.

Name: *Paracheirodon axelrodi*, Cardinal Tetra, subfamily Tetragonopterinae

Location and Natural Habitat: Mainly Rio Negro and its tributaries, Brazil. Inhabits quiet, sluggish creeks, rivers with aquatic vegetation, and tree-shaded lakes.

Adult Size: 2 inches (5 cm).

Minimum Aquarium Size: 15 gallons (55 L).

Husbandry Requirements: Prefers soft (dH <5), acidic (pH 5.5 to 6.5) water. A peaceful, active species best maintained in a school of at least eight with its own kind.

Diet: Aquatic insect larvae and crustaceans in the wild. Offer commercially prepared aquarium foods, both dry and frozen. Supplement diet with live brine shrimp, mosquito larvae, and daphnia.

Reproduction: Keep pH (6.0 to 6.5), and dH <5. Will spawn among java moss or spawning mops on the bottom of the aquarium. Remove

The Cardinal Tetra (Paracheirodon axelrodi) *is one of the most attractive and popular characins.*

Paragoniates alburnus, *also known as the Pasca Tetra, is an unusually shaped, rare characin.*

parents after spawning. Offer juveniles infusoria and green water as first foods.

Name: *Paracheirodon innesi,* Neon Tetra, subfamily Tetragonopterinae

Location and Natural Habitat: Widespread in the Peruvian Amazon. Inhabits quiet, sluggish creeks and rivers with aquatic vegetation.

Adult Size: 1.75 inches (4 cm).

Minimum Aquarium Size: 15 gallons (55 L).

Husbandry Requirements: Prefers soft (dH <5), acidic (pH 6.0 to 7.0) water. A peaceful, active species best maintained in a school of at least eight with its own kind.

Diet: Aquatic insect larvae and crustaceans in the wild. Offer commercially prepared aquarium

The popular Neon Tetra (Paracheirodon innesi) *commands a strong following and can be found in virtually all tropical fish establishments.*

foods, both dry and frozen. Supplement diet with live brine shrimp, mosquito larvae, and daphnia.

Reproduction: pH 6.0 to 6.5, and dH <5. Will spawn among java moss or spawning mops on the bottom of the aquarium. Remove parents after spawning. Offer juveniles infusoria and green water as first foods.

Name: *Paragoniates alburnus,* Pasca Tetra, subfamily Paragoniatinae

Location and Natural Habitat: Venezuela and the Amazon River basin, Brazil. Inhabits small creeks and rivers with moderately flowing water over aquatic vegetation.

Adult Size: 3 inches (7.5 cm).

Minimum Aquarium Size: 40 gallons (150 L).

Husbandry Requirements: Water chemistry unimportant. Provide open space, since it is an active swimmer. A peaceful species best maintained with other nonaggressive species of similar size.

Diet: Omnivorous in the wild. Offer a varied diet consisting of commercially prepared dried and frozen foods. Supplement the diet with live brown worms, mosquito larvae, daphnia, and bloodworms.

Reproduction: Unknown. Has not yet spawned in captivity.

This Red-Bellied Pacu (**Piaractus brachy-pomum**) *is often mistaken for the Red-Bellied Piranha by hobbyists as well as fish and game personnel.*

Name: *Piaractus brachypomus*, Red-Bellied Pacu, subfamily Serrasalminae
Location and Natural Habitat: Amazon River Basin. Inhabits large, slow-flowing rivers in open water as well as flooded forests during the rainy season.
Adult Size: 18 inches (45 cm).
Minimum Aquarium Size: 150 gallons (600 L).
Husbandry Requirements: Water chemistry unimportant. Provide plenty of open space, as this species is an active swimmer. Best maintained in a small school or with other large, nonaggressive species.
Diet: Omnivorous in the wild. Offer a varied diet consisting of commercially prepared dried and frozen foods. Supplement the diet with inexpensive aquatic plants.
Reproduction: Unknown. Has not yet spawned in captivity.

Name: *Pristella maxillaris*, Pristella Tetra, subfamily Tetragonopterinae
Location and Natural Habitat: Amazon River basin throughout northern South America. Inhabits small creeks to large, slow-flowing rivers.
Adult Size: 1.75 inches (4.5 cm).

Minimum Aquarium Size: 15 gallons (55 L).
Husbandry Requirements: Water chemistry unimportant. A peaceful, active species best maintained in a school of at least eight or with other tiny, peaceful aquarium fish.
Diet: Aquatic insect larvae in the wild. Offer commercially prepared aquarium foods, both dry and frozen. Supplement diet with live brine shrimp, mosquito larvae, and daphnia.
Reproduction: Great beginner characins to start out with. Water chemistry not critical for spawning. Will spawn among java moss or spawning mops on the bottom of the aquarium. Remove parents after spawning. Offer juveniles infusoria and green water as first foods.

Name: *Pygocentrus cariba*, Black-Shoulder Piranha, subfamily Serrasalminae
Location and Natural Habitat: Venezuela and Guyana. Inhabits nearly all types of aquatic habitats.
Adult Size: 12 inches (30 cm).
Minimum Aquarium Size: 150 gallons (600 L).
Husbandry Requirements: Water chemistry unimportant. A robust, nervous species that will feel more at ease if maintained in a school of its own kind or with other *Pygocentrus* or

The Pristella Tetra (**Pristella maxillaris**) *is a desirable characin, with most of its chromatic appeal concentrated in its fins. A small school makes for a very pleasing sight.*

Most piranhas, like this **Pygocentrus cariba,** *show attractive metallic colors over the body.*

The best-known species of piranha is the Red-Bellied Piranha, **Pygocentrus nattereri.**

Serrasalmus species. Do not maintain with smaller peaceful species unless plenty of hiding places are offered.

Diet: Mammal carrion and fish in the wild. Offer raw fish, beef heart, and whole shrimp.

Reproduction: Lower pH to 7.0, dH <10, and reduce lighting. Spawns in pairs. Provide several spawning mops as a spawning medium. Remove adults afterward, or remove spawning mops with eggs to a separate aquarium. Eggs hatch out in eight days and can be fed newly hatched brine shrimp as a first food.

Name: *Pygocentrus nattereri,* Red-Bellied Piranha, subfamily Serrasalminae

Location and Natural Habitat: From Guyana southwards to Brazil and northern Argentina. Inhabits primarily white-water habitats.

Adult Size: 12 inches (30 cm).

Minimum Aquarium Size: 150 gallons (600 L).

Husbandry Requirements: Water chemistry unimportant. A robust, nervous species that will feel more at ease if maintained in a school of its own kind or with other *Pygocentrus* or *Serrasalmus* species. Do not maintain with smaller peaceful species unless plenty of hiding places are offered.

Diet: Mammal carrion and fish in the wild. Offer whole fish, beef heart, and whole shrimp.

Reproduction: Lower pH to 7.0, dH <10, and reduce lighting. Spawns in pairs. May construct a circular nest in the substrate and guard eggs and fry. Eggs hatch out in eight days and can be fed newly hatched brine shrimp as a first food.

Name: *Pygocentrus piraya,* Black-Tailed Piranha, subfamily Serrasalminae

Location and Natural Habitat: Rio Sao Francisco basin, eastern Brazil. Inhabits nearly all types of aquatic habitats.

Adult Size: 16 inches (40 cm).

Minimum Aquarium Size: 200 gallons (750 L).

*The Black-Tailed Piranha (***Pygocentrus piraya***) is one of the rarest piranhas in the hobby, and usually commands a high price.*

Husbandry Requirements: Water chemistry unimportant. A robust, nervous species. This species will feel more at ease if maintained in a school of its own kind or with other *Pygocentrus* or *Serrasalmus* species. Do not maintain with smaller peaceful species unless plenty of hiding places are offered.

Diet: Mammal carrion and fish in the wild. Offer raw fish flesh, beef heart, and whole shrimp.

Reproduction: Unknown. Has not yet spawned in captivity.

Name: *Rhoadsia altipinna,* subfamily Rhoadsiinae

Location and Natural Habitat: Ecuador and Western Columbia. Inhabits cool, slow-flowing rivers in open water.

Adult Size: 7 inches (17.5 cm).

Minimum Aquarium Size: 80 gallons (300 L).

Husbandry Requirements: Water chemistry unimportant. A robust, hardy, and active swimming species best maintained with other large, aggressive species. Do not maintain with smaller, peaceful species as they will be preyed upon.

Diet: Piscivorous in the wild. Offer high-protein foods such as live feeder guppies, fresh shrimp, frozen foods, and pellets.

Due to its aggressive disposition, **Rhoadsia altipinna** *can be kept with larger, more aggressive species.*

This unusual Central American characin (**Roeboides bouchellei**) *is not often seen in the hobby. It is occasionally brought in by enterprising hobbyists who travel to Central America.*

Reproduction: Condition adults on live foods. Water chemistry unimportant. Lower temperature to 72°F (22°C). Provide a sandy bottom, as the male will construct a shallow depression as a spawning site. The male will protect eggs and young. Young can be left with the male, or the adults should be removed to another aquarium. Juveniles are large enough to accept live baby brine shrimp as a first food.

Name: *Roeboides bouchellei,* subfamily, Characinae

Location and Natural Habitat: Costa Rica to Panama. Inhabits most small to moderately sized river systems.

Adult Size: 6 inches (15 cm).

Minimum Aquarium Size: 50 gallons (190 L).

Husbandry Requirements: Water chemistry unimportant. A sedentary species that is best maintained by itself or with larger, aggressive species too large to be swallowed. Do not maintain with smaller, peaceful species as they may be consumed or descaled.

Diet: Piscivorous as well as scale eating in the wild. Offer high-protein foods such as live feeder guppies, fresh shrimp, frozen foods, and pellets.

Reproduction: Unknown. Has not yet spawned in captivity.

Name: *Salmimus maxillosus,* Dorado, subfamily Bryconinae

Location and Natural Habitat: The Rio De La Plata basin. Inhabits large rivers and lakes.

Adult Size: 3 feet (90 cm).

Minimum Aquarium Size: 500 gallons (1,900 L).

Husbandry Requirements: Water chemistry unimportant. An aggressive species best maintained with other large, aggressive fish. Keep interior of aquarium sparsely decorated as this species needs a lot of swimming space. Do not maintain with any fish small enough to be considered as food.

Diet: Piscivorous in the wild. Offer live feeder fish supplemented with freshly frozen, high-protein foods.

Reproduction: Unknown. Has not yet spawned in captivity.

Name: *Serrasalmus geryi,* Gery's Piranha, subfamily Serrasalminae

Location and Natural Habitat: Tocantins River, Brazil. Inhabits nearly all types of aquatic habitats.

The Dorado (**Salmimus maxillosus**) *grows to a length of 3 feet (1 m). At this size, it takes on a beautiful golden coloration over the entire body.*

Gery's Piranha (**Serrasalmus geryi**) *is one of the more unusually shaped and attractive piranhas to have recently been exported from South America.*

Adult Size: 8 inches (20 cm).

Minimum Aquarium Size: 100 gallons (375 L).

Husbandry Requirements: Water chemistry unimportant. Not as aggressive as most piranhas. Will feel more at ease if maintained in a school of its own kind or with other *Pygocentrus* or *Serrasalmus* species. Do not maintain with smaller peaceful species unless plenty of hiding places are offered.

Diet: Mammal carrion and fish in the wild. Offer raw fish flesh, beef heart, and whole shrimp.

Reproduction: Unknown. Has not yet spawned in captivity.

Name: *Serrasalmus cf. spilopleura,* Blackband Piranha, subfamily Serrasalminae

Location and Natural Habitat: Amazon River basin, Orinoco River basin, and Rio De La Plata basin. Inhabits nearly all types of aquatic habitats.

Adult Size: 10 inches (25 cm).

Minimum Aquarium Size: 100 gallons (375 L).

Husbandry Requirements: Water chemistry unimportant. This species will feel more at ease

The Blackband Piranha (Serrasalmus cf. spilopleura) sports a more elongated anal fin than most piranhas.

if maintained in a school of its own kind or with other *Pygocentrus* or *Serrasalmus* species. It is not advisable to house this species with other non-meat-eating Serrasalmids.

Diet: Mammal carrion and fish in the wild. Offer raw fish flesh, beef heart, and whole shrimp.

Reproduction: Unknown. Has not yet spawned in captivity.

Name: *Thayeria obliqua*, Penguin Tetra, subfamily Tetragonopterinae

Location and Natural Habitat: Madeira River system of Brazil. Inhabits quiet, sluggish creeks and rivers with aquatic vegetation.

Adult Size: 3 inches (7.5 cm).

Minimum Aquarium Size: 20 gallons (75 L).

Husbandry Requirements: Water chemistry unimportant. A peaceful, active species best maintained in a school of at least six or with other tiny, peaceful aquarium fish.

Diet: Aquatic insect larvae in the wild. Offer commercially prepared aquarium foods, both dry and frozen. Supplement diet with live brine shrimp, mosquito larvae, and daphnia.

Reproduction: Unknown. Has not yet spawned in captivity.

Name: *Triporthus angulatus*, Dusky Elongate Hatchetfish, subfamily Bryconinae

Location and Natural Habitat: Amazon River basin. Inhabits small, quiet rivers with overhanging vegetation.

Adult Size: 9 inches (22.5 cm).

Minimum Aquarium Size: 40 gallons (150 L).

Husbandry Requirements: Water chemistry unimportant. Decorations should consist of submerged wood, smooth stones, and aquatic plants. A peaceful species best maintained with other nonaggressive species of similar size.

Diet: Insectivorous in the wild. Offer commercially prepared dried and frozen foods

The Penguin Tetra (Thayeria obliqua) typically swims in a tail-down, head-up position.

Even though the Dusky Elongate Hatchetfish (Triportheus angulatus) looks similar to the actual Hatchetfishes, it is nonetheless more closely related to the preceding species.

supplemented with live brine shrimp, fruit flies, daphnia, mosquito larvae, and brown worms.

Reproduction: Unknown. Has not yet spawned in captivity.

Family Chilodontidae

Name: *Chilodus gracilis,* Black-Banded Headstander

Location and Natural Habitat: Amazon River basin. Inhabits quiet, sluggish creeks and rivers with aquatic vegetation.

Adult Size: 5 inches (12.5 cm).

Minimum Aquarium Size: 30 gallons (110 L).

Husbandry Requirements: Water chemistry unimportant. A peaceful, sluggish species best maintained with other similar-sized, peaceful aquarium fish.

Diet: Omnivorous in the wild. Offer commercially prepared dried and frozen foods. Supplement diet with algae wafers and live brine shrimp, mosquito larvae, brown worms, and daphnia.

Reproduction: Unknown. Has not yet spawned in captivity.

Family Crenuchidae

Name: *Characidium cf. fasciatum,* Darter Tetra, subfamily Characidiinae

Location and Natural Habitat: Rio Negro, Brazil. Tends to inhabit slow-moving or lentic water.

Adult Size: 4 inches (10 cm).

Minimum Aquarium Size: 30 gallons (110 L).

Husbandry Requirements: Water chemistry unimportant. A lively, active species best maintained in a community aquarium of similar-sized fish. Provide plenty of current and several smooth stones.

Diet: Aquatic insect larvae and crustaceans in the wild. Offer commercially prepared aquarium

As the common name implies, the Black-Banded Headstander (Chilodus gracilis) *typically orients itself in a head-down position.*

It is difficult to separate many Darter Tetra species of the genus Characidium, *such as this* C. cf. fasciatum, *because many look very similar to each other.*

foods, both dry and frozen. Supplement diet with live brine shrimp, mosquito larvae, and daphnia.

Reproduction: Unknown. Has not yet spawned in captivity.

Name: *Characidium* sp., Hummingbird Darter Tetra, subfamily Characidiinae

Location and Natural Habitat: Amazon River basin. Tends to inhabit slow-moving or lentic water.

Adult Size: 2 inches (5 cm).

Minimum Aquarium Size: 15 gallons (55 L).

Husbandry Requirements: Water chemistry unimportant. A lively, active species best maintained in a community aquarium of similar-sized fish. Provide gentle current and several smooth stones.

This **Characidium** *species was seen to spend much of its time hovering in mid-water, and was given the common name of Hummingbird Darter Tetra.*

Diet: Aquatic insect larvae and crustaceans in the wild. Offer commercially prepared aquarium foods, both dry and frozen. Supplement diet with live brine shrimp, mosquito larvae, and daphnia.

Reproduction: Unknown. Has not yet spawned in captivity.

Name: *Characidium cf. rachovii,* subfamily Characidiinae

Location and Natural Habitat: Southeast Uruguay. Inhabits small creeks with profuse aquatic vegetation.

Adult Size: 2.25 inches (6 cm).

Minimum Aquarium Size: 15 gallons (55 L).

The author collected this **Characidium cf. rachovii** *from the Rio San Juan, Colonia, Uruguay. Note the attractively patterned anal fin of this male. This Darter Tetra prefers cooler water than most species, thriving at temperatures ranging from 68°F to 72°F (20°C to 22°C).*

The **Sailfin Tetra** **(Crenuchus spilurus)** *is one of only a few characin species that practice a degree of parental care of their young.*

Husbandry Requirements: Water chemistry unimportant. Prefers cool water between 65°F and 72°F (18°C and 22°C). A lively, active species best maintained in a community aquarium of similar-sized fish. Provide plenty of current and several smooth stones.

Diet: Aquatic insect larvae and crustaceans in the wild. Offer commercially prepared aquarium foods, both dry and frozen. Supplement diet with live brine shrimp, mosquito larvae, and daphnia.

Reproduction: Unknown. Has not yet spawned in captivity.

Name: *Crenuchus spilurus,* Sailfin Tetra, subfamily Crenuchinae

Location and Natural Habitat: Peru and Brazil. Found in quiet, black-water habitats with overhanging plant roots, submerged tree trunks, branches, and aquatic vegetation.

Adult Size: 2.5 inches (6.5 cm).

Minimum Aquarium Size: 20 gallons (75 L).

Husbandry Requirements: Water chemistry unimportant. A somewhat aggressive, active species best maintained in a community aquarium of similar-sized fish. Provide plenty of submerged wood and live plants.

Diet: Aquatic insect larvae and crustaceans in the wild. Offer a varied diet of commercially prepared aquarium foods, both dry and frozen.

Supplement diet with live brine shrimp, mosquito larvae, and daphnia.

Reproduction: Maintain pH between 6.0 to 6.5, and dH <5. Will spawn among the hollow recesses of submerged wood. Some parental care provided. Offer juveniles infusoria and green water as first foods.

Name: *Poecilocharax weitzmani*, Weitzman's Tetra, subfamily Crenuchinae

Location and Natural Habitat: Rio Negro, Brazil. Inhabits quiet, sluggish creeks and rivers with overhanging plant roots, submerged tree trunks, branches, and aquatic vegetation.

Adult Size: 2 inches (5 cm).

Minimum Aquarium Size: 20 gallons (75 L).

Husbandry Requirements:. Maintain pH between 6.0 to 6.5, and dH <5. A somewhat aggressive species best maintained in a community aquarium of similar-sized fish. Provide plenty of submerged wood and live plants. A delicate species.

Diet: Aquatic insect larvae in the wild. Offer commercially prepared aquarium foods, both dry and frozen. Supplement diet with live brine shrimp, mosquito larvae, and daphnia.

Reproduction: Maintain water chemistry the same as for general maintenance. Will spawn among the hollow recesses of submerged wood. Some parental care noted. Offer juveniles infusoria and green water as first foods.

Family Ctenoluciidae

Name: *Boulengerella maculata*, Spotted Pike Characin

Location and Natural Habitat: Amazon River basin. Inhabits the quieter parts of moderate to large rivers.

Adult Size: 15 inches (45 cm).

Poecilocharax weitzmani is known to spawn in the hollow recesses of submerged branches.

Minimum Aquarium Size: 100 gallons (375 L).

Husbandry Requirements: Water chemistry unimportant. Provide plenty of open space. A placid species that will not molest fish too large to be swallowed whole. Do not maintain with any other fish less than half its size.

Diet: Piscivorous in the wild. Offer live minnows, shiners, or guppies as food.

Reproduction: Unknown. Has not yet spawned in captivity.

Name: *Ctenolucius beani*, Central American Pike Characin

Location and Natural Habitat: From Panama to Columbia. Inhabits the open waters of rivers and swamps.

Adult Size: 12 inches (30 cm).

Minimum Aquarium Size: 75 gallons (300 L).

The Spotted Pike Characin (Boulengerella maculata) reaches a length of 15 inches (37.5 cm), thus making them suitable only for large aquariums.

This Central American Pike Characin (Ctenolucius beani) was collected in Southern Panama by renowned aquarist Stan Sung.

Husbandry Requirements: Water chemistry unimportant. Provide plenty of open space. A placid species that will not molest fish too large to be swallowed whole. Do not maintain with any other fish less than half its size.

Diet: Piscivorous in the wild. Offer live minnows, shiners, or guppies as food.

Reproduction: Unknown. Has not yet spawned in captivity.

Family Curimatidae

Name: *Curimata* sp., Dwarf Sabado

Location and Natural Habitat: Rio San Juan, Colonia, Uruguay. Inhabits small creeks with profuse aquatic vegetation.

Adult Size: 5 inches (12.5 cm).

The author collected this obscure Curimatid (Curimata sp.) Dwarf Sabado from the Rio San Juan, Colonia, Uruguay.

Minimum Aquarium Size: 40 gallons (150 L).

Husbandry Requirements: Prefers cool water between 65°F and 72°F (18°C to 22°C). Water chemistry unimportant. Inoffensive and retiring, so provide plenty of hiding places such as submerged wood and tough aquatic plants.

Diet: Herbivorous and detritivorous. Offer foods high in vegetable content such as spirulina flakes and algae wafers.

Reproduction: Unknown. Has not yet spawned in captivity.

Family Cynodontidae

Name: *Cynodon gibbus,* Fathead Wolf Tetra, subfamily Cynodontinae

Location and Natural Habitat: Amazon River basin. Inhabits slow-flowing rivers in open water.

Adult Size: 12 inches (30 cm).

Minimum Aquarium Size: 200 gallons (750 L).

Husbandry Requirements: Water chemistry unimportant. Sedentary, yet easily excited; provide plenty of open space. A peaceful species toward fish too small to be consumed. Best maintained with other nonaggressive species of similar size.

The Fathead Wolf Tetra (Cynodon gibbus) is one of the more recently imported Wolf Tetras to be made available to the hobby.

Diet: Piscivorous in the wild. Offer feeder guppies, minnows, or shiners.
Reproduction: Unknown. Has not yet spawned in captivity.

Name: *Gilbertolus alatus,* Dwarf Biting Tetra, subfamily Roestinae
Location and Natural Habitat: The Rio Magdalena in Columbia and the Maracaibo basin of Venezuela. Inhabits sluggish creeks and small rivers.
Adult Size: 5 inches (12.5 cm).
Minimum Aquarium Size: 55 gallons (210 L).
Husbandry Requirements: Water chemistry unimportant. Decorations should consist of submerged wood and ample aquatic plants. A peaceful, nervous species best maintained with other nonaggressive species of similar size. Quite delicate and easily injured by handling and netting.
Diet: Surface-dwelling insects and aquatic insect larvae in the wild. Offer commercially prepared dried and frozen foods supplemented with live daphnia, mosquito larvae, and wingless fruitflies.
Reproduction: Unknown. Has not yet spawned in captivity.

Name: *Hydrolycus pectoralis,* Wolf Tetra, subfamily Cynodontinae
Location and Natural Habitat: Amazon River basin in Brazil and Bolivia. Inhabits slow-flowing rivers in open water.
Adult Size: 15 inches (45 cm).
Minimum Aquarium Size: 100 gallons (375 L).
Husbandry Requirements: Water chemistry unimportant. Sedentary, yet easily excited; provide plenty of open space. A peaceful species toward fish too small to be consumed. Best maintained with other nonaggressive species of similar size.

Gilbertolus alatus is occasionally imported mixed with shipments of Silver Hatchetfishes.

The Wolf Tetra (Hydrolycus pectoralis) is a highly specialized characin that will only feed on small fishes.

Diet: Piscivorous in the wild. Offer feeder guppies, minnows, or shiners.
Reproduction: Unknown. Has not yet spawned in captivity.

Family Erythrinidae
Name: *Erythrinus* sp., "Peru"
Location and Natural Habitat: Peruvian Amazon. Inhabits sluggish creeks and small rivers among leaf litter.
Adult Size: 12 inches (30 cm).
Minimum Aquarium Size: 100 gallons (375 L).
Husbandry Requirements: Water chemistry unimportant. Highly predaceous and aggressive. Maintain only with fish twice their size or larger. Provide plenty of hiding places. Somewhat quarrelsome among themselves.

This attractive Erythrinus *sp. from Peru stands out as the most colorful member of the family Erythrinidae. Males have brighter colors and longer dorsal fins.*

Diet: Piscivorous in the wild. Offer feeder guppies, minnows, or shiners.
Reproduction: Unknown. Has not yet spawned in captivity.

Name: *Hoplias malabaricus,* Wolf Fish
Location and Natural Habitat: Amazon River basin. Found in virtually every habitat, including rivers, lakes, creeks, and small muddy ponds.
Adult Size: 2 feet (60 cm).
Minimum Aquarium Size: 250 gallons (950 L).
Husbandry Requirements: Water chemistry unimportant. Highly predaceous and aggressive. Maintain only with fish twice their size or larger. Provide plenty of hiding places. Somewhat quarrelsome among themselves. Large specimens can inflict a serious bite on the unwary aquarist. A nocturnal species.

The Wolf Fish (Hoplias malabaricus), *like all Erythrinids, is predatory and will devour any fish small enough to fit into its mouth. Tankmates must be chosen with great care.*

The Marbled Hatchetfish (Carnegiella strigata) *is a smaller, less hardy Hatchetfish than its larger, silvery-colored cousins.*

Diet: Piscivorous in the wild. Offer feeder guppies, minnows, or shiners.
Reproduction: Has only recently been spawned in captivity.

Family Gasteropelecidae
Name: *Carnegiella strigata,* Marbled Hatchetfish
Location and Natural Habitat: Peruvian and Brazilian Amazon. Inhabits quiet creeks and small rivers nearshore.
Adult Size: 2 inches (5 cm).
Minimum Aquarium Size: 15 gallons (55 L).
Husbandry Requirements: Maintain pH between 6.5 to 7.0, and dH <5. A peaceful, active species best maintained in a school of at least six or with other tiny, peaceful aquarium fish. Keep lid tightly closed as this species is a jumper.
Diet: Surface-dwelling insects in the wild. Offer commercially prepared dried and frozen foods supplemented with live daphnia, mosquito larvae, and wingless fruitflies.
Reproduction: Will spawn among spawning mops or the dangling roots of water hyacinth at the surface. Remove parents after spawning. Offer juveniles infusoria and green water as first foods.

Thoracocharax securis comes highly recommended for the novice characin hobbyist. It is hardy, undemanding, and peaceful.

Name: *Thoracocharax securis,* Silver Hatchetfish

Location and Natural Habitat: Central Amazon River basin. Inhabits swift-flowing rivers.

Adult Size: To 3.5 inches (9 cm).

Minimum Aquarium Size: 30 gallons (110 L).

Husbandry Requirements: Water chemistry unimportant. A peaceful, active species best maintained in a school of at least six with its own kind or with other peaceful aquarium fish. Keep lid tightly closed as this species is a jumper.

Diet: Surface insects in the wild. Offer commercially prepared dried and frozen foods supplemented with live daphnia, mosquito larvae, and wingless fruitflies.

Reproduction: Unknown. Has not yet spawned in captivity.

Family Hemiodontidae

Name: *Hemiodopsis gracilis,* Redtail Hemiodus

Location and Natural Habitat: Guyana and Brazil. Inhabits open waters of most river systems.

Adult Size: To 6 inches (15 cm).

Minimum Aquarium Size: 75 gallons (300 L).

Husbandry Requirements: Water chemistry unimportant. Provide open space, as this species is an active swimmer. A peaceful, active species

Hemiodopsis gracilis is the only Hemiodontid to be regularly exported for the aquarium trade.

best maintained with other nonaggressive species of similar size.

Diet: Filamentous algae, plankton, and aquatic insect larvae in the wild. Offer commercially prepared dried and frozen foods that include spirulina supplemented with live daphnia and mosquito larvae.

Reproduction: Unknown. Has not yet spawned in captivity.

Family Lebiasinidae

Name: *Copella nattereri,* Natterer's Copella, subfamily Pyrrhulininae

Location and Natural Habitat: Amazon River basin within Brazil. Inhabits small creeks with profuse aquatic vegetation.

When it comes time to spawn, both male and female Natterer's Splashing Tetra (Copella nattereri) will jump from the water onto a nearby leaf to lay their eggs before leaping back into the water.

Adult Size: To 2 inches (5 cm).

Minimum Aquarium Size: 15 gallons (55 L).

Husbandry Requirements: Maintain pH between 6.5 to 7.0, and dH <5. A peaceful, active species best maintained in a school of at least six with its own kind or with other tiny, peaceful aquarium fish.

Diet: Aquatic insect larvae in the wild. Offer commercially prepared dried and frozen foods supplemented with live daphnia and mosquito larvae.

Reproduction: Lays eggs on broad-leaved aquatic plants. Remove parents after spawning. Offer juveniles infusoria and green water as first foods.

Name: *Lebiasina boruca,* subfamily Lebiasininae

Location and Natural Habitat: Costa Rica. Inhabits small to medium, swift-flowing rivers.

Adult Size: To 5 inches (12.5 cm).

Minimum Aquarium Size: 50 gallons (190 L).

Husbandry Requirements: Water chemistry unimportant. Active swimming species requiring an aquarium with few decorations. Maintain with other species of similar size. Will prey upon small fish.

Diet: Piscivorous and insectivorous in the wild. Offer commercially prepared dried and frozen foods high in protein. Supplement the

This **Lebiasina boruca** *was collected in Costa Rica by famed aquarist John Neimans.*

Nannobrycon eques *swims in a head-up, tail-down position typical for pencilfish species of the genus* **Nannobrycon.**

diet with live brown worms, mosquito larvae, daphnia, and bloodworms.

Reproduction: Unknown. Has not yet spawned in captivity.

Name: *Nannobrycon eques,* Eques Pencilfish, subfamily Pyrrhulininae

Location and Natural Habitat: Amazon River basin within Peru and Brazil. Inhabits small, shaded creeks and streams with over-hanging terrestrial vegetation, submerged leaves, small branches, and other such debris.

Adult Size: To 2 inches (5 cm).

Minimum Aquarium Size: 15 gallons (55 L).

Husbandry Requirements: Maintain pH between 6.5 to 7.0, and dH <5. A peaceful, active species best maintained in a school of at least six or with other tiny, peaceful aquarium fish.

Diet: Aquatic insect larvae in the wild. Offer commercially prepared dried and frozen foods supplemented with live daphnia and mosquito larvae.

Reproduction: Only a single pair required. Should be provided with dense aquatic vegetation throughout most of the aquarium. Eggs released among the plants. Remove parents after spawning. Offer juveniles infusoria and green water as first foods.

Name: *Nannostomus espei,* Espei Pencilfish, subfamily Pyrrhulininae

Location and Natural Habitat: Southwest Guyana. Inhabits small, shaded creeks and streams with overhanging terrestrial vegetation, submerged leaves, small branches, and other such debris.

Adult Size: To 1.75 inches (4.5 cm).

Minimum Aquarium Size: 15 gallons (55 L).

Husbandry Requirements: Maintain pH between 6.5 to 7.0, and dH <5. A peaceful, active species best maintained in a school of at least six or with other tiny, peaceful aquarium fish.

Diet: Aquatic insect larvae in the wild. Offer commercially prepared dried and frozen foods supplemented with live daphnia and mosquito larvae.

Reproduction: Only a single pair required. Should be provided with dense aquatic vegetation throughout most of the aquarium. Eggs released among the plants. Remove parents after spawning. Offer juveniles infusoria and green water as first foods.

Name: *Nannostomus cf. marginatus,* Coral Red Pencilfish, subfamily Pyrrhulininae

Location and Natural Habitat: Rio Nanay and Rio Tigre, Peru. Inhabits small, shaded creeks and streams with overhanging terrestrial

Pencilfishes of the genus **Nannostomus,** *such as these* **Nannostomus espei,** *swim in a horizontal fashion.*

The Coral Red Pencilfish (**Nannostomus cf. marginatus**) *is one of the most exciting new characin discoveries from the Peruvian Amazon.*

vegetation, submerged leaves, small branches, and other such debris.

Adult Size: To 1.5 inches (3.5 cm).

Minimum Aquarium Size: 15 gallons (55 L).

Husbandry Requirements: Maintain pH between 6.0 to 6.5, and dH <4. A peaceful, active species best maintained in a school of at least six or with other tiny, peaceful aquarium fish.

Diet: Aquatic insect larvae in the wild. Offer commercially prepared dried and frozen foods supplemented with live daphnia and mosquito larvae.

Reproduction: Only a single pair required. Should be provided with dense aquatic vegetation throughout most of the aquarium. Eggs released among the plants. Remove parents after spawning. Offer juveniles infusoria and green water as first foods.

Name: *Nannostomus trifasciatus,* Three-Lined Pencilfish, subfamily Pyrrhulininae

Location and Natural Habitat: Southern Amazon River basin. Inhabits small, shaded creeks and streams with overhanging terrestrial vegetation, submerged leaves, small branches, and other such debris.

The Three-Lined Pencilfish (Nannostomus trifasciatus), typical of most pencilfishes, requires soft, acidic water for long-term successful care.

This undescribed Pyrrhulina sp. from the Amazon River basin in Brazil is indicative of just how attractive some of the pencilfish relatives can be.

Adult Size: To 2.5 inches (6 cm).
Minimum Aquarium Size: 20 gallons (75 L).
Husbandry Requirements: Maintain pH between 6.5 to 7.0, and dH <5. A peaceful, active species best maintained in a school of at least six or with other tiny, peaceful aquarium fish.
Diet: Aquatic insect larvae in the wild. Offer commercially prepared dried and frozen foods supplemented with live daphnia and mosquito larvae.
Reproduction: Only a single pair required. Should be provided with dense aquatic vegetation throughout most of the aquarium. Eggs released among the plants. Remove parents after spawning. Offer juveniles infusoria and green water as first foods.

Name: *Pyrrhulina* sp., subfamily Pyrrhulininae
Location and Natural Habitat: Peruvian Amazon. Inhabits small creeks with profuse aquatic vegetation.
Adult Size: To 3 inches (7.5 cm).
Minimum Aquarium Size: 30 gallons (110 L).
Husbandry Requirements: Water chemistry unimportant. A peaceful, active species best maintained in a school of at least six with its own kind or with other tiny, peaceful aquarium fish.

Diet: Aquatic insect larvae in the wild. Offer commercially prepared dried and frozen foods supplemented with live daphnia and mosquito larvae.
Reproduction: Spawns on submerged leaves. Male guards eggs until hatching. Offer newly hatched juveniles green water and infusoria as first foods.

Family Parodontidae
Name: *Parodon* sp., South American Flying Fox
Location and Natural Habitat: Columbia, Ecuador, and Peru. Inhabits swift-flowing rivers over algae-covered stones.
Adult Size: To 4 inches (10 cm).

This South American Flying Fox of the genus Parodon shows up from time to time in dealers' aquariums. They appear to be the South American equivalent to the Asian cyprinid (Crossocheilus siamensis).

Minimum Aquarium Size: 40 gallons (150 L).

Husbandry Requirements: Water chemistry unimportant. Requires a well-oxygenated aquarium with many smooth stones scattered about. Provide strong current. A peaceful, active species best kept by itself or with other peaceful species.

Diet: Algae and aquatic insects in the wild. Offer commercially prepared dried and frozen foods that include spirulina supplemented with live daphnia, brown worms, and mosquito larvae.

Reproduction: Unknown. Has not yet spawned in captivity.

Name: *Saccodon dariensis*

Location and Natural Habitat: Panama to Columbia. Inhabits swift-flowing rivers over algae-covered stones.

Adult Size: To 6 inches (15 cm).

Minimum Aquarium Size: 50 gallons (190 L).

Husbandry Requirements: Water chemistry unimportant. Requires a well-oxygenated aquarium with many smooth stones scattered about. Provide strong current. A peaceful, active species best kept by itself or with other peaceful species.

Diet: Algae and aquatic insects in the wild. Offer commercially prepared dried and frozen foods that include spirulina supplemented with live daphnia, brown worms, and mosquito larvae.

Reproduction: Unknown. Has not yet spawned in captivity.

Family Prochilodontidae

Name: *Semaprochilodus taeniurus*, Flagtail Prochilodus

Location and Natural Habitat: Amazon River basin. Inhabits most river systems with a variety of habitats.

Adult Size: To 15 inches (38 cm).

This rare **Saccodon dariensis**, *collected by Stan Sung from swift-flowing rivers south of the Panama Canal, requires a high oxygen content and strong current in order to be successfully maintained in captivity.*

Minimum Aquarium Size: 150 gallons (600 L).

Husbandry Requirements: Water chemistry unimportant. Do not maintain with aquatic plants. Can be kept with other aquarium fish, regardless of size, so long as they have a peaceful disposition.

Diet: Diatoms and microorganisms from submerged branches, stones, and so forth in the wild. Offer commercially prepared foods, both dried and frozen, with a high concentration of vegetable matter such as algae or spirulina.

Reproduction: Unknown. Has not yet spawned in captivity.

The Flagtail Prochilodus (**Semaprochilodus taeniurus**) *makes for an impressive show fish in a large aquarium, particularly as a full-sized adult.*

INFORMATION

Glossary

Adipose fin: A fleshy, usually rayless fin, located on the back of certain fish, behind the dorsal fin and in front of the caudal fin

Carnivore: a living organism's natural habitat

Cryptic: camouflage; an animal with a color pattern that mimics the color or shape of its habitat

Ctenoid scale: circular scale with several small, pointed projections on its outer edge

Cycloid scale: circular scale with smooth edges all around

Detritivore: an animal that eats organic waste

Endemic: restricted to a specific place

Herbivorous: a plant-eating animal

Heterotrophic bacteria: bacteria capable of using various organic materials for their food and energy needs

Insectivore: an animal that eats insects and or their larvae

kH: carbonate hardness; the measurement of the amount of carbonate, or bicarbonate, in water

Lateral line: a series of receptors embedded in the scales of a fish that can usually be seen as a narrow line running horizontally down the body; these receptors enable the fish to detect nearby movement in the water

Lentic: Pertaining to or living in still water

Monophyletic: a group of related organisms derived from a common ancestor

pH: a value on the scale of 0 to 14 that indicates the acidity or alkalinity of water; acidic water has a pH less than 7, and alkaline water has a pH higher than 7

Pharyngeal teeth: teeth located in the throat that aid in the mastication of food

Pheromone: a chemical substance released by an animal that serves to influence the physiology or behavior of other members of the same species

Phytoplankton: microscopic plants and free-floating algae suspended in the water column

Piscivore: an animal that eats fish

Planktivore: an animal that eats free-floating phytoplankton and zooplankton

Zooplankton: tiny aquatic animals, usually crustaceans and insect larvae, that float in the water

Useful Literature

Magazines

Tropical Fish Hobbyist
TFH Publications, Inc.
211 West Sylvania Avenue
Neptune, NJ 07753
908-988-8400

Aquarium Fish Magazine
Fancy Publications, Inc.
Subscription Department
P.O. Box 53351
Boulder, CO 80323-3351

Hatchetfishes, such as this Carnegiella marthae, *are capable of limited "flight" just above the surface of the water.*

Journals

Ichthyological Explorations of Fresh Waters
Dr. Friedrich Pfiel
P.O. Box 65 00 86
D-81214, München, Germany

Books

Fairfield, T. *A Commonsense Guide to Fish Health,* Hauppauge, New York: Barron's Educational Series, Inc., 2000.

Malabarba, L. R., R. E. Reis, R. P. Vari, Z. M. Lucena, and C. A. S. Lucena, eds. *Phylogeny and Classification of Neotropical Fishes,* Porto Alegre, Brazil: Edipcrs., 1998.

Gery, J. *Characoids of the World*, Neptune, New Jersey: TFH Publications, Inc., 1977.

Breder, Charles M., D. E. Rosen. *Modes of Reproduction in Fishes*, Neptune, New Jersey: TFH Publications, Inc., 1966.

Baensch, H. A., G. W. Fischer. *Aquarium Atlas Photo Index 1-5*, Melle, Germany: Mergus, 1997.

Book Dealers

Aquatic Book Shop
P.O. Box 2150
Shingle Springs, CA 95682-2150
530-622-7157
http://www.seahorses.com

Finley Aquatic Books
150 North Road
Pascoag, RI 02859
Tel: 401-568-0371
Fax: 401-568-1561

Important Notes

Electrical equipment for aquarium care is described in this book. Please do not fail to read the note below, since otherwise serious accidents could occur.

Water damage from broken glass, overflowing, or tank leaks cannot always be avoided. Therefore, you should not fail to take out insurance.

Please take special care that neither children nor adults ever eat any aquarium plants. It can cause serious health injury. Fish medication should be kept away from children.

Safety Around the Aquarium

Water and electricity can lead to dangerous accidents. Therefore, you should make absolutely sure when buying equipment that it is suitable for use in an aquarium.

• Every technical device must have the UL sticker on it. These letters give the assurance that the safety of the equipment has been carefully checked by experts and that "with ordinary use" (as the experts say) nothing dangerous can happen.

• Always unplug any electrical equipment before you do any cleaning around or in the aquarium.

• Never do your own repairs on the aquarium or the equipment if there is something wrong with it. As a matter of safety, all repairs should only be carried out by an expert.

Dedication

To Matthew Bahnsen, my first nephew and fellow heir in Christ.

Acknowledgments

The author wishes to thank the following people who, over the years, offered their unyielding hospitality and access to their ideas, theories, or fish to photograph. Many have given of their time to help me understand various perplexing and complicated concepts and ideas. My deepest apologies if I have inadvertently omitted those who have figured in any way to my growing knowledge of characins.

Jim Bellissimo of Jim's Exotic Fish, Dr. Warren Burgess, Jim and Agnus Forshey, Pat Brokaw of Southland Aquatics, Phil Farrel, Kjell Fohrman, Stuart Grant, Vinny Kutty, Scott and Bruce Lapham of Pet Town Tropical Fish, John Lombardo, Oliver Lucanus's generous contribution of rare South American characin photographs, Kevin Luker and the gang at Poseidon Aquatics in Los Angeles, Steve Lundblad of the Cichlid Exchange who sent me unusual and rare species to photograph, Steve Lundblad of Dolphin International for access into the inner sanctum, Ken Childs—keeper of the inner sanctum of Dolphin International and for all his generous help and incredible knowledge of fish, John Neimans—who graciously helped to house my wild-caught Uruguayan characins back in 1997, Michel and Clotilde Perbost, Ben Rosler, David Schleser of Natures Images for his careful review of the initial manuscript and for his numerous suggestions and corrections, Dick Strever, Stan Sung who offered his photo of *Saccodon dariensis*—the first person ever to photograph this species alive and in color, Dr. Weitzman of the Smithsonian Museum of Natural History for his wisdom, advice, and research materials generously given, Jerry Walls, and Wesley Wong.

Cover Photos

Mark Phillip Smith.

Photo Credits

Oliver Lucanus: pages 2–3, 61 (left), 89; Stan Sung: page 91; Mark Phillip Smith: all other photos.

About the Author

Mark Phillip Smith is a professional wildlife photographer, explorer, and discoverer of freshwater temperate and tropical fishes. In 1990, he contributed to the discovery of a genus and two species of Lake Malawi Cichlids. In 1994, he discovered several new species of cichlids in Lake Edward, Uganda. His ichthyological interests have taken him to Japan, Mexico, Uruguay, Malawi, Zambia, Zimbabwe, Kenya, Uganda, England, Sweden, Hawaii, and the Caribbean. He writes for domestic and international publications, and lectures widely on the cichlids of Lake Tanganyika and Lake Malawi.

All inquiries should be addressed to:
Barron's Educational Series, Inc.
250 Wireless Boulevard
Hauppauge, NY 11788
http://www.barronseduc.com

Library of Congress Catalog Card No. 2001056685

ISBN-13: 978-0-7641-2148-7
ISBN-10: 0-7641-2148-0

Library of Congress Cataloging-in-Publication Data
Smith, Mark Phillip, 1966–
    Tetras and other characins : everything about history, setting up an aquarium, health concerns, and spawning / Mark Phillip Smith ; illustrations by Michele Earle-Bridges.
        p. cm.
    Includes bibliographical references (p.).
    ISBN 0-7641-2148-0
        1. Tetras. 2. Characidae. 3. Aquarium fishes. I. Title.

SF458.T4 S65 2002
636.3'748—dc21   2001056685

Printed in China

9 8 7 6 5 4 3 2